LEADERSHIP THROUGH
HELL
AND HIGH
WATER

A Leader's Guide to
Crisis Management

Jean-Marc Guillamot

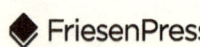 FriesenPress

One Printers Way
Altona, MB R0G 0B0
Canada

www.friesenpress.com

ISBN
978-1-03-916880-0 (Hardcover)
978-1-03-916879-4 (Paperback)
978-1-03-916881-7 (eBook)

1. BUSINESS & ECONOMICS, FREELANCE & SELF-EMPLOYMENT

Distributed to the trade by The Ingram Book Company

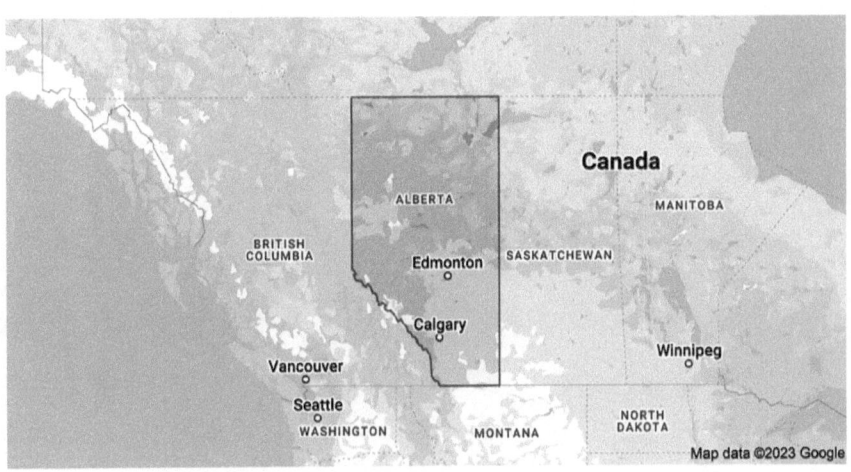

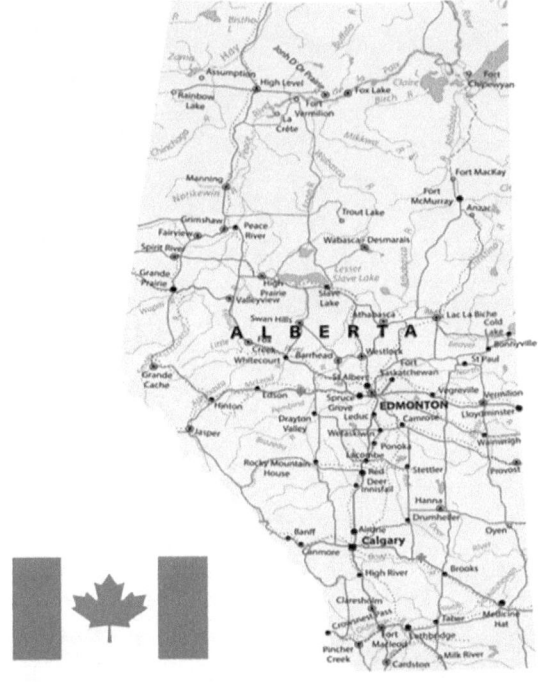

Table of Contents

Dedication

I dedicate this book to my family: Donna, my courageous and always supportive wife; Monique, my adventurous, multi-talented daughter and Daniel, my always "driven to succeed" son.

I will also add the wonderful assistance of Team Wone's team leaders! They are aware of who they are!

Finally, I thank all emergency responders from all agencies involved in natural or human-caused tragedies around the world for their daily unselfish actions and sacrifices.

Preface

Everyone remembers where they were and what they were doing during momentous events, whether they were international, national, or personal. The moon landing, JFK's assassination, September 11, 2001, terrorist attacks on the twin towers, left emotional scars on us all. Some incidents were devastating, while others were joyful, but they all had an impact on how we respond in times of crisis. Nowadays, the world is moving from crisis to crisis, and we are striving to cope with their escalating severity and destructive trajectory.

Many studies have been undertaken on various crises and their psychological effects on those who see or participate in them. This book is not designed to address the question of how to "abort a crisis," but rather to provide individuals with basic disciplines and techniques for crisis management based on my personal and historical experiences.

In this book, I will use two key incidents that had immediate personal consequences for me. The word "Hell" in the title refers to the wildfires that raged in Fort McMurray, Alberta, beginning on May 1, 2016. The fire burned 2,400 homes and buildings, displaced 86,000 people in three communities, and cost $9.9c. billion in damages, making it the most expensive disaster in Canadian history.[1]

"High Water" portrays a once-in-a-century flood event that occurred in the same city. On April 26, 2020, the local rivers inundated the hamlet due to the many unmanageable ice packs developing in the riverbed. COVID-19 exacerbated the chaos, imposing further strain on the populace. I was the leader of a group of eight hotels and staff throughout these two key

---

1   "2016 Fort McMurray Wildfire," Wikipedia, accessed October 16, 2023, https://en.wikipedia.org/wiki/2016_Fort_McMurray_wildfire.

occasions, and I confronted unpredictable conditions in both cases while directing teams and navigating through these risky, turbulent waters. During those trying times, I was eternally grateful for the love and support from my wife, family, coworkers, and friends.

When thrown in the middle of flames or faced with surging water flows, there is no book or guidebook on how to deal with such terrible situations. You react and adjust. Leaders and leadership will triumph, even though some will be overwhelmed, depending on how they manage these unique conditions. If you must take a book with you in times of trouble, I hope you choose mine.

I authored this book by combining my experience and lessons learned to present best practices for dealing with disasters. I provide readers with a personal path to becoming equipped with basic crisis management tactics while in a position of leadership. A leader does not have to be a general, CEO, or mayor. As I demonstrate in these pages, leadership is a duty that people choose to accept throughout their lives rather than a position or rank.

Everyone has the potential to be a leader. There is a widely held belief that leaders are born leaders. But it is truly a matter of choice and strong will when people choose to step up and lead! Throughout this book, we shall return to this fundamental concept. Can anyone be a crisis leader? Crisis leadership, according to American academic Andrew J. DuBrin, "is the process of leading group members through a circumstance considered largely unanticipated, intensely negative, and emotionally draining."[2]

Every crisis and situation is unique, and everyone will manage and oversee a crisis in diverse ways. Most catastrophes are sudden and unpredictable. In this book, I have outlined several lists on diverse topics to assist readers in reflecting on and how to act should similar circumstances present themselves.

---

2   Kathya N. Nordin, "Making Sense of Leaders' Perceptions about Effectiveness in Communication during a Crisis," (Master thesis, Mid Sweden University, 2020), 11, http://www.dportal.org/smash/get/diva2:1535125/FULLTEXT01.pdf.

Introduction

Borrowing from the maritime world, I have added some very personal logs to this book. These reflect on moments when I, and many others, went through hell with the wildfires and high water during the devastating floods which hit our city. This first personal log, however, introduces me.

Personal Log: Casablanca, Morocco, 1952 to 1968

I was born and raised in Casablanca, Morocco, by my French parents, who loved me very much. My upbringing exposed me to two contrasting worlds: a French, Catholic self-imposed inclusion and a dynamic, adventurous atmosphere anchored in a rigorous Muslim society that embraced the European way of life while preserving its roots in art, cuisine, and history. While growing up, I learned to be resourceful, a trait that has helped me throughout my career by listening and showing respect when interacting with people from diverse religious and social backgrounds.

My mother's culinary skills were exceptional, and my father was a gracious host who entertained guests at our home. As a result, it exposed me to the catering industry at a very young age. My mother and I would visit the souk *market, where she taught me how to select the freshest products and negotiate the price as per tradition. This ritual had a significant impact on my future, as I am not one to maintain the status quo.*

When I was born, phones were still the clunky, charcoal-black boxes that rang loudly on desks, walls, or counters. In Casablanca, owning a TV was a luxury. We mostly relied on selected and censored magazines and a Philips transistor radio for global news. Because of Morocco's temperate weather, outdoor activities and sports were commonplace. My parents enrolled me in the Sea Scouts at an early age, where I learned to sail on old French navy barges called cara-vels. Our group of seven sailors traversed on a twenty-eight-foot-long ketch with two masts and three sails. We learned the "ropes" of sailing by understanding and practising knots, sailing manoeuvres, and wind knowledge. GPS was nonexistent back then, so we relied on compasses, navigational maps, and sextants for navigation.

Our leaders challenged each "équipe" to undertake rigorous on-sea challenges to earn a coveted badge, confirming our sea knowledge and worthiness at sea. In December 1967, our leader gave my team the challenge of sailing from Casablanca to Tenerife, located to the west of Africa. The trip covered about 550 nautical miles and took the entire 3 weeks of the Christmas period. We sailed first to Mogador, now called Essaouira, to replenish our food and water before setting sail towards Tenerife. We ended up being early as winds favoured us in coasting along the North African shores, and our spirits were high.

However, a few days after leaving Mogador, the winds were more closed haul, which required constant repositioning in relation to our Tenerife destination. We had a walkie-talkie device that enabled constant communication with our chaperone who followed us in his own boat.

On the fourth day, after leaving Mogador late in the afternoon, we started seeing ominous clouds on the horizon. The warm winds from the Sahara and the wintry winds from the Atlantic could suddenly develop into Alize winds with dramatic consequences. Our chap-erone, who had radio equipment aboard his ship, warned us of an incoming storm. The sea and Mother Nature have their own rules, and their moods will always be the biggest challenges sailors face. In our case, we only had basic training in sailing in rough weather. But going through it in exercises, as opposed to being tossed, drenched, and thrown overboard without mercy, was a different story than what the manual said. Our chef d'équipe started to panic and shut down, not abiding by the basic rules of navigation under such severe circumstances. Storm tactics help manage a storm once you are in it. There are various tried-and-true options, all of which try to lessen strain and motion by pointing one of the boat's ends (either the bow or stern) towards the waves. Having lost his ability to think clearly, our chef did not abide by the major rule of going against the waves as opposed to letting the rudder go.

At around 8:00 p.m., we capsized. All of us were in shock, but our chef d'équipe was even more stuporous. He could not speak. Unknowingly, I took charge. Later, I will explain how the subconscious takes over, but there is a correlation between deep personal survival instinct, the understanding of the situation and circumstances you are suddenly facing, and how we can survive with the resources on hand and benefit from others when thrown into a crisis. These are the fundamentals of leading under crisis which I will explore in this book.

As soon as I got a sense of the situation we were facing, I immediately directed the team's focus on getting the maximum amount of fresh drinking water stored in yellow jerry cans, most of which were attached under benches and some floating around us. You can survive without food but not without fresh water, whether you are at sea or on land. While we still had the most energy, I instructed my teammates to dive and collect some of our canisters, secured and stored as emergency supplies under the hull. The boat was then "turtling," in navigational terms, with the hull facing the sky.

The sudden storm that hit us subsided quickly, but we lost sight of our chaperone and lost our walkie-talkies. Stranded and capsized in the open sea, we climbed atop the overturned hull and waited for rescue. Hypothermia was the most significant risk we faced, especially in cold water. Thankfully because of the Gulf Stream transporting heat from the Gulf of Mexico across the Atlantic towards

Europe, the water was at an average of 20°C in the area where we capsized. Furthermore, the full moon offered us some visibility.

As we were still running on adrenaline in the first few hours, I suggested we try to right the boat using cables and ropes still attached to the masts. Some of us climbed onto the hull and attempted to pull up the mast to balance the boat with the sea.

However, we soon realized it was better to conserve our energy. We huddled together on the hull and organized watches, water rations, and other necessities, ensuring our physical and mental well-being was prioritized. .

While we waited to be rescued, we shared stories and jokes, supporting each other through the challenging situation. Our chef d'équipe slowly recovered from his shock, and I encouraged everyone to focus on our collective predicament, rather than individual concerns. We were fortunate that none of us suffered serious injuries, although our lips became extremely chapped from early stages of dehydration, we managed by rationing our water supply. The weather was moderate—not too hot or cold—but the wind remained strong in the early part of the day. As the first light of day emerged, the sea calmed. We had five emergency flares, but I urged my colleagues to wait until daylight, as we were following the shipping lanes towards Tenerife when we capsized.

Around 4:00 p.m. the following day, we spotted a couple of boats in the distance. In the clear, blue sky, we fired three of our emergency flares in succession. Shortly after, we saw two fishing boats veering towards us at top speed, coming to our rescue. Our chaperone's boat had sustained considerable damage, with a broken rudder and a split on the main mast that had forced him to drift away from us. Instead of trying to reach us, our rescuer headed towards the nearest island, Fuerteventura, part of the Canary Islands archipelago. He enlisted the aid of local Spanish and Portuguese fishermen in the search for us and saving our lives.

This encounter had a great impression on me, and I still think about it today. It gave me important lessons about how to lead people and stay effective in times of crisis.

During the COVID-19 pandemic, many of us had personal difficulties, and I am certain that we are all exhausted by our own struggles to the point that speaking or reading about them gets monotonous. Unfortunately, crises are on the horizon. We are doomed to face the realities of climate-related crises, and the future bears the uncertain possibility of further pandemics or unanticipated natural or human-caused disasters.

Crises can occur abruptly, with warnings of oncoming calamity being rejected by leaders, particularly at the highest levels of an institution. Leaders must be prepared to make key decisions in the face of significant uncertainty. The reality for individuals in positions of authority is that they will eventually face a severe occurrence or crisis affecting themselves, the people working for and with them, and others close to them.

Leading during extreme disasters requires managers to make important judgments in the face of tremendous uncertainty while completing complicated organizational tasks to protect lives and property. Managers must act decisively while being adaptable to rapidly changing threats to the environment. A hierarchical command-and-control structure is sufficient for managing activities in most ordinary emergencies. However, during extreme crises, such a command structure is frequently insufficient and may even inhibit inter-organizational response.

Leaders in times of crisis must combine a vertical command-and-control approach with a horizontal network capable of connecting, collaborating, and coordinating with others. In a crisis, the ability to build networks for information exchange and flatten the command structure for collaboration is crucial.. These crisis leadership ideas are applicable to any organization confronted with challenging, complex, and novel circumstances.

Extreme events transcend authorities and overwhelm a single organization's ability to manage the crisis alone. Leaders must devise methods that will allow their organizations to adjust to these occurrences. Crisis leaders need to quickly build a network that lets people connect, work together, and coordinate with each other along with a vertical command-and-control system for running their company.

By fostering information-sharing networks, leaders can ensure that crucial information is quickly disseminated among team members, enabling them to make informed decisions and take swift action. Additionally, breaking down conventional command structures allows for a more agile and collaborative approach to crisis management, empowering team leaders to adapt and respond effectively to rapidly evolving situations.

Leaders must swiftly learn how to navigate through unpredictable and tricky situations, frequently with scarce information. They must be able to determine what is most important and design an action plan accordingly. While there may be tension, strong leaders may preserve a feeling of hope and courage by including everyone around them in navigating the waves of change and information. They must accept their own as well as others' mistakes and grow in self-confidence as they lead. Despite the difficulties, crises can lead to self-development and respect for personal and professional relationships. To preserve their people's support, leaders must be daring, honest, and communicate effectively.

Crisis leadership ideas can be utilized in both commercial and government settings, as well as any situation in which organizations must manage hard, complex, and unprecedented events.

Crisis leaders who are ahead of the curve should give their companies not only standard emergency procedures but also strategies that can be used in a variety of situations. Organizations, like individuals, use the crisis environment to build their own ideals, much like we do in our own lives. Leadership is constantly self-analyzing, evaluating strengths, flaws, vulnerabilities, and opportunities.

Like all of us, I never want my everyday environment and routines to be upended, but during a crisis, events beyond my control require me to continuously review my own identity as well as the identities of the groups I head.. While I would never desire more challenges in anyone's life, going through a crisis has surely helped me develop survival and self-confidence skills, all while appreciating the support of my closest personal relationships and business contacts.

In his book *Consider the Lobster and Other Essays,* David Foster Wallace says, "A real leader is somebody who can help us overcome the limitations of our own individual laziness and selfishness and weakness and fear and get us to do better things than we can get ourselves to do on our own."[3]

Leaders are created by the repetition of important behaviours that get ingrained in their subconscious, triggered by internal chemicals and a desire to overcome uncertainty, danger, and collective dread.

During a crisis, leaders are frequently under enormous pressure to act swiftly, find instant solutions, and make decisions. The larger the issue, however, the less likely a leader will be able to quickly manage the situation. Leaders must remove themselves from emotional and practical urgency to focus on precise measures that will have a meaningful impact.

In today's ever-changing world, crises have become all too common. I hope this book will teach readers how to pivot in such situations. I outline several best practices that may be useful in both personal and professional settings. These tips should help individuals adapt quickly and effortlessly during stressful and unpredictable periods, which may be extremely difficult for both them and their colleagues.

Crisis leadership is complicated and multidimensional. Leaders will face extreme difficulties, from personal issues to life-and-death decisions, and their abilities will be evaluated in ways they never imagined. People will analyze and critique their ideas, conduct, and deeds. It is critical to remember that crisis leadership has a dramatic impact on all individuals engaged, not only now but also in the future.

Leadership is a deliberate manifestation of who you are, what you do, and how you do it. It is critical to keep things simple during a crisis since the mind can easily become overwhelmed with information and diversions. While numerous books on leadership exist, only a handful specifically cover crisis leadership. Considering the regularity and severity of crises in our world today, it is critical to investigate and comprehend the response mechanisms for individuals and organizations alike.

This book emphasizes the "human" approach to crisis leadership rather than the control of materialistic goods. While these guidelines may

---

3   Maria Popova, "David Foster Wallace on Leadership, illustrated and read by Debbie Millman," accessed on January 5, 2024. https://www.themarginalian.org/2014/02/17/ dfw-leadership-debbie-millman/#:~:text=In%20other%20words%2C%20a%20 real,to%20do%20on%20our%20own.

improve material assets, their primary purpose is to avoid uncertainty and frustration during crises, which can inflict more damage on companies and teams in already difficult circumstances.

The latest pandemic has affected us all. We must face the truth that we are also dealing with a climate catastrophe that is causing harm and human misery. No one knows what the future holds in terms of potential pandemics ni.

Crisis in History

I have great admiration for several historical personalities, military leaders, and scientists whom I have modestly quoted while researching their crisis leadership skills and best practices.

Leaders such as President Abraham Lincoln and Prime Minister Winston Churchill had great abilities in managing many crises at the same time. They inspired their people to maintain hope and fight for their values while also being brutally honest about the circumstances.

Lincoln faced the daunting task of leading the country through the American Civil War, one of the deadliest and most controversial conflicts in American history. He demonstrated strong leadership by proclaiming martial law, suspending the writ of habeas corpus, and issuing the Emancipation Proclamation. He also worked relentlessly to maintain the Union's support, visiting troops on the front lines, and delivering speeches that galvanized the nation to fight on. Significant disagreements arose within Lincoln's administration, particularly between Secretary of State William Seward and Secretary of War Edwin Stanton. Despite this, he kept control of his administration and managed the opposing personalities efficiently. Following the Civil War, Lincoln faced the difficult challenge of rebuilding the country and reconciling with the Confederacy. He pushed for a more fair and just society by supporting the Thirteenth Amendment, which ended slavery, and by championing policies that helped rebuild the South.

Winston Churchill is widely considered one of history's greatest crisis leaders, particularly for his leadership during World War II, and was noted for his tenacity and drive. Throughout his career, he endured numerous losses, including political defeats, personal problems, and military combat failures. Despite these obstacles, he remained focused on his objectives and never gave up. He was a gifted communicator who utilized his oratory abilities to mobilize the British people during the war. He delivered several memorable speeches that enthused and energized the nation, including his "We Shall Fight on the Beaches" address in 1940.

Churchill was an analytical thinker who could see the big picture and make difficult choices. He was not hesitant to take chances, such as the choice to continue fighting after France fell, even if it put Britain in jeopardy.

Despite his commanding nature, Churchill could work well with others. He collaborated closely with other Allied leaders, including Franklin D. Roosevelt and Joseph Stalin, to coordinate military strategy to secure the war effort's success. Churchill was an expert in crisis management, and he oversaw unforeseen occurrences and emergencies with poise and assurance. He dealt decisively and unwaveringly with the Blitz bombings of London and other British cities, as well as the prospect of Nazi Germany's invasion.

Overall, history has shown us that effective crisis leadership necessitates a blend of inspiration, drive, and honesty. Churchill's example demonstrates that during hardship, leaders must be able to articulate their vision and motivate their followers to be resilient, even in the most demanding situations.

One such example is Winston Churchill's motivating statements during a prospective Nazi invasion, in which he urged and motivated his compatriots to remain hopeful despite the oncoming threat. "We shall not fail or falter; we shall not weaken or tire," Churchill said emphatically. "Neither the sudden shock of battle, nor the long-drawn trials of vigilance and exertion will wear us down."[4] "Give us the tools, and we will complete the job" became a rallying cry for the British people. He gave another rousing speech to the House of Commons on June 4, 1940, exemplifying the need to be "brutally honest" by spelling out the situation as clearly as possible: "We shall fight in France, we shall fight on the seas and oceans, we shall

---

4   F. B. Czarnomski, ed., The Wisdom Of Winston Churchill (London: Allen & Unwin, 1956), https://archive.org/stream/in.ernet.dli.2015.425596/2015.425596.The-Wisdom_djvu.txt.

fight with growing confidence and growing strength in the air, we shall defend our Island, whatever the cost may be, we shall fight on the beaches, we shall fight on the landing grounds, we shall fight in the fields and in the streets, we shall fight in the hills; we shall never surrender."[5]

Historians and biographers have spent a lot of time debating Lincoln's leadership; however, a remarkable quality that I have read and admired in such remarkable books as *Teams of Rivals: The Political Genius of Abraham Lincoln* by Doris Kearns Goodwin and *Lincoln* by David Herbert Donald is his unwavering determination to complete his mission. Despite the many obstacles and objections, he faced, he remained focused on his personal agenda. This discipline allowed him to persevere during critical times of crisis. He skillfully used his own personal time of introspection, which I call "me time," to balance periods of reflection and decisive action, which served him well and ultimately benefited the United States. I consider him to be a self-made leader rather than a superhuman. He learned through experience and committed himself to self-improvement while enhancing his intelligence and emotional awareness. As he went through problems, failures, and disappointments, he turned them into chances to strengthen his resolve to succeed for the good of everyone. Abraham Lincoln had a keen sense of his own mental and physical capabilities. He is an excellent role model for those who desire to lead with dignity and ethics even when situations and circumstances get difficult to overcome.

Franklin D. Roosevelt, a prominent American president, displayed outstanding leadership during the banking crisis by advising Americans to retain their funds in banks. FDR's bravery and unwavering determination in challenging situations, together with his readiness to take prompt action during emergencies, were among of his most prominent characteristics.

As the American civil rights movement gained traction in the late 1950s and early 1960s, Reverend Martin Luther King Jr. urged his followers to participate in sit-ins, marches, and other forms of protesting racial

---

5   Kristin Hunt, "Winston Churchill's Historic 'Fight Them on the Beaches' Speech Wasn't Heard by the Public Until After WWII," Smithsonian Magazine, November 21, 2017, https://www.smithsonianmag.com/history/winston-churchills-historic-fight-them-beaches-speech-wasnt-heard-public-until-after-wwii-180967278/#:~: text=%E2%80%9CWe%20shall%20fight%20in%20France,in%20the%20streets%2C%20 we%20shall.

discrimination. His stance was firm, and he refused to hide the truth, pushing leaders to be open to tough conversations and not just accept what had been done.

On a smaller scale, Ernest Shackleton's leadership during the Antarctic exploration is a perfect example of "Us through Hell and High Water." When his expedition ship, *Endurance*, became trapped in the ice, Shackleton insisted that each man maintain their duties.

This routine and manual labour helped establish order and grounded the crew during uncertain and dangerous times. Shackleton displayed remarkable adaptability in the face of ever-evolving challenges, seamlessly transitioning his primary objective from exploration to the critical pursuit of survival. When their ship became uninhabitable, he promptly directed his crew to construct a makeshift camp on the unforgiving ice. He and a select few embarked on an audacious journey, traversing a staggering eight hundred miles aboard a lifeboat to reach another island with the hope of securing assistance. After an arduous four-month odyssey, Shackleton triumphantly returned to the initial island, discovering to his profound relief that his entire team had defied the odds and endured.

Maintaining a sense of humour can contribute to psychological resilience. It does not mean ignoring the seriousness of the crisis, but rather finding a way to navigate through it with a positive mindset. Resilience allows people to adapt, bounce back, and continue moving forward, even in the face of adversity. President Zelenskyy of Ukraine faced an extraordinary challenge when a Russian army was advancing towards the capital, Kyiv. In response to an offer of support to evacuate the city, Zelenskyy, on February 26, 2022, on the footsteps of his government house targeted by Russia, galvanized his people by stating, "I need ammunition, not a ride."

Abraham Lincoln was a great storyteller and he used it to the benefit of friends and associates capturing stories and anecdotes he collected in the backwoods of Illinois.

Churchill was a great raconteur, and he delighted his audience with short quips such as: "In the course of my life, I have often had to eat my words, and I must confess that I have always found it a wholesome diet."[6] And while attending Roosevelt's regular celebratory cocktail hours, he was heard saying, "I am ready to meet my Maker. Whether my Maker is prepared for the great ordeal of meeting me is another matter."[7]

6   Quote research, "During My Life I Have Often Had too Eat My Own Words, and I Have Found Them a Wholesome Diet," Quote Investigator, December 5, 2022, https://quoteinvestigator.com/2022/12/05/wholesome/.

7   "Winston Churchill Quotes." Quotes.net. STANDS4 LLC, accessed January 8, 2024, <https://www.quotes.net/quote/11951>.

Part One:
"Me" Through "Hell And High Water"

"ME" and the Beginning of a Crisis

Personal Log: Fort McMurray, Alberta, May 3, 2016: Through Hell!

From Morocco, I embarked on my lifelong career by attending a hotel school in Nice, France, for three years. This rigorous training provided me with a solid foundation in the hospitality industry. I further honed my skills by working in England, Germany, and Switzerland before immigrating to Canada as a birthday gift to myself in April 1975. Initially posted in a hotel in Montreal for the hotel management company Atlific, whom I later crossed paths with many years later in Fort McMurray, Alberta. I transferred to Halifax, where I met my wife Donna and started a family with our daughter Monique and son Daniel. Climbing the ladder of the hotel industry, I held executive positions in various locations across the country, from Cape Breton and Moncton to Quebec, British Columbia, and finally Alberta.

In 2007, they posted me to Fort McMurray, Alberta, a town that was never on my bucket list. The initial dynamics of the city, fuelled by the surge in exploiting the oil sands, provided me with an extraordinary challenge. With the support of my family and a resolute team, I managed eight hotel properties, which I progressively acquired over a few years.

Fast forward to Sunday, May 1, 2016. I was relaxing on the patio with my wife, enjoying the unseasonably beautiful, clear, blue sky, when we noticed a plume of smoke on the west side of our townhouse. Initially, we assumed it would be quickly extinguished; however, the smoke grew over the next few hours. Listening to the local radio, we learned about an active forest fire that crews were trying to control. As the evening unfolded, the air became thick with the smell of burning wood and the sky turned ominous. Precautionary measures resulted in some houses on the west side of town being evacuated.

Waking up on the morning of May 2, we learned from radio stations and social media sites that the situation had come under control after partial evacuations of some nearby housing complexes.

Wood Buffalo Fire Chief Darby Allen led his team in battling what he would later call "the Beast" for its ferocity, unpredictability, and extensive reach. On the morning of May 2, Allen said the fire was much closer to Fort McMurray, but they were still hopeful they could contain it.

There was a lot of smoke in the air, and the sky was cloudy, but I was comforted to hear that the previous evacuation orders were now reduced to shelter-in-place. By then, the winds were blowing the fire away from the city. At around 5:30 p.m., as heard on the local station 100.3 Cruz FM, Fire Chief Allen stated, "We hope we can stop this fire before it gets into town."

Despite smelling burnt wood and still seeing a dimmed flame on the west and north sides looking over our patio, my wife and I went to bed around 10:30 p.m. We heard Allen's last words as "All things considered; it is looking good. But I worry that if the wind changes direction, we are still in a perilous situation." We hoped for the best.

On May 3, at 7:30 a.m., I drove downtown to the Clearwater Suite Hotel for work. I started my day by calling all my hotel managers to ask if everyone was okay and to please stay close to their cell phones. The sky had a shot of blue between heavy smoke when looking to the north, but smoke was visible on the south side of town. I asked all maintenance managers of our properties to close up the air units on the roofs of our hotels to prevent too much smoke from entering the building for the comfort of guests and team members.

I had a previously scheduled lunch with a client at one of our properties, the Radisson Hotel, located south of town. But during lunch, I got continuous texts from my general managers reflecting their concerns about team members having to evacuate their families and homes. Social media channels were inundated with words of anxiety from citizens about the safety of their families, especially kids at school, while parents were working at the oil sand sites, which were on average one and a half hours out of town. I sped up to finish my lunch.

As I stepped outside the Radisson Hotel, I was met with a thick, dark cloud looming over the residential Beacon Hill development just across from our property. I immediately instructed my second-in-command, Mike Harlick, a hotel manager for one of our properties, to be on standby for the evacuation of all guests and team members. I asked Mike to relay the same message to all general managers and to direct housekeeping to knock on room doors to ensure everyone was informed. I asked for immediate maintenance tasks to be completed, such as closing all the air vents, moving gas cylinders left outside of kitchens, and clearing underground parking lots.

In a rush, I drove down to our downtown properties, starting with the Franklin Suite Hotel. I informed the general manager of the situation and instructed them to begin the same process as at the Radisson. As I left the property, I was confronted by a wall of flames coming across the main highway on Abasand, another suburban development on a hill.

Philippe Gadbois, one of our VPs based in Toronto, called to express his concern about what he had heard on the national news. I confirmed our common concerns and mentioned that if the fires jumped the Athabasca River, we were in deep trouble. Unbeknownst to me, this had already occurred thirty minutes prior to the call.

However, around 4:00 p.m., all hope was lost when the fire took a turn towards the town, separating the downtown and north parts of town and spreading rapidly. The city administrators and fire department evacuated both the residential areas of Beacon Hill and Abasand, but things quickly worsened as the fire approached the water treatment plant needed to fight the blaze.

That was the day we evacuated all of Fort McMurray. The original plan was to send everyone south, but it quickly became apparent that the road system could not manage the load. The Regional Emergency Operations Centre (REOC) split the city, sending twenty thousand to twenty-five thousand evacuees north and sixty thousand south. Fire Chief Allen was really concerned that we would lose a considerable number of lives and a major amount of property.

These were the early hours of what would become the most expensive disaster in Canadian history, with damages estimated at $10 billion, displacing 86,000 inhabitants on short notice (about 4 hours), and spanning 590,000 hectares.[8]

Although no one was killed directly by the fire, two young individuals escaping the flames were sadly killed in an automobile accident. I knew this would be a day I would never forget, and that I would have to take charge and lead amid the turmoil and unpredictable circumstances.

Our actions—and inactions—are a direct effect of the wiring of our brains. Neuroscientists are continuously discovering how our brains behave. They make advances and discoveries about how the human brain functions and heals, as well as how its mechanisms influence human behaviour and memory.

Because of experience, the brain evolves in both structure and function. It is not a rigid organ, and it responds to how we teach it. I liken my brain to an ATM bank machine. The more "intellectual" money I put in, the more money or mental resources I can withdraw when I need them.

Understanding our brain and the key players during times of stress is critical to understanding how and why we react in crisis situations. The brain is a curious organ that controls our responses, both good and bad. If panic is our default reaction to a crisis, we can empower ourselves with skills to help us overcome this gut reaction. During stressful times, the

---

8   "2016 Fort McMurray Wildfire," Wikipedia, accessed on November 13, 2023, https://en.wikipedia.org/wiki/2016_Fort_McMurray_wildfire.

brain is flooded with information from both our internal and external environments. It detects patterns and analyzes this information using cognitive biases, which are preconceived conceptions created by culture, prior experience, and desire, influencing our perceptions of circumstances and actions.

Imagine delving into the depths of your mind, navigating the intricate corridors of your brain, and stumbling upon a modest yet influential figure: the amygdala. This unassuming almond-shaped entity resides within the expansive territory of the limbic system, reigning over the realm of emotions. Think of it as your brain's vigilant sentry, poised to unleash a piercing alarm when danger looms.

When the tides of circumstance take a treacherous turn, the amygdala springs into action, igniting a chain reaction that echoes the primeval instincts of our ancestors. It is like an internal fire panel, finely tuned to detect threats before our conscious awareness even has a chance to awaken. There is an almost mystical quality to this sentinel, as if it is attuned to a frequency that eludes our consciousness —a frequency that resonates with imminent peril.

Mitroff Crisis Management founder and President Ian Mitroff devised a model that separates crisis management into five stages: signal detection, probing and prevention, damage containment, recovery, and learning.[9]

To paraphrase Mitroff's principles, and because I work in the hotel industry, let us compare the brain to a standard hotel floor layout. You gather your operating and material resources on the lower floor or basement. This is where you would find hotel supplies, a storeroom, spare equipment, and machinery. When people are threatened, instinctively the brain begins here to gather resources and prepare to battle (signal detection). The cerebral temporal and occipital lobes control smell, sight, memory, speech, and hearing, and are like the main lobby level of a hotel where the action happens and where scents, sounds, and crowds generate a buzz that parades through the lobby. The primary fire panel

9   Studocu, Mitroff's Theory Theory on Crisis Management, accessed January 8, 2024. https://www.studocu.com/ph/document/ateneo-de-naga-university/strategic-management/theoretical-framework/39747787.

of the majority of buildings and hotels is situated in the lobby (probing and prevention), enabling immediate awareness of the location where problems are occurring. The administration offices and rooms are on the higher floor, as are the cerebrum's parietal and frontal lobes, which control personality, thinking, planning, problem-solving, and senses (damage containment). It focuses on executive thought, processing, and introspection (sleep, recovery, and learning).

What truly captivates my curiosity is how the amygdala assumes command in these critical moments. It becomes a conductor of a grand symphony, orchestrating the compliance of other brain regions. Even the prefrontal cortex, the sanctuary of our logical reasoning, can find itself yielding to the amygdala's influence.

The amygdala yields a dual role of power and obligation. It serves as the catalyst for our primal instincts, and the "fight, flight, or freeze" response, a survival mechanism etched into our very essence. Yet, here is the twist: our modern world, with all its complexities, often challenges the alignment of this response with the nuanced situations we encounter. Our amygdala may occasionally sound its alarm bells without due cause, momentarily sidelining our capacity for thoughtful decision-making.

Thus, within the intricate circuitry of our brain's machinery, the amygdala emerges as both a guardian and a potential disruptor. It is a vivid reminder of our ancestry, juxtaposed against the intricate demands of our contemporary existence.

This hijacking can elicit strong emotional responses and hamper our capacity to think clearly and respond properly. The amygdala is responsible for the processing and assessment of emotional cues such as fear, anger, happiness, and sadness. It aids in the detection and identification of emotional stimuli from the environment, allowing for speedy emotional responses.

Daniel Kahneman, a Nobel Prize-winning psychologist, describes in his 2011 bestselling book *Thinking Fast and Slow,* two systems at work in the brain: one slow and one quick.[10]

---

10   Daniel Kahneman, "Fast and Slow Thinking," ModelThinkers, accessed October 31, 2023, https://modelthinkers.com/mental-model/fast-and-slow-thinking?type=share.

System one functions automatically and swiftly, requiring little or no effort and displaying no sense of intentional control. Routine or reactive circuits, such as lifting your hand out of a scorching oven, are rapid circuits. The speedy response produces hormones such as cortisol and adrenaline, which impact physical well-being, breathing rate, oxygen intake, and blood delivery to the muscles and prepares the body for fight, flight, or freeze. While the amygdala's speed and efficacy are both a blessing and a curse. It is critical to develop self-control to prevent making harsh decisions with long-term consequences. You complete these tasks through familiarity or repetition, training them in your subconscious.

System two, on the other hand, is the deliberate, slow, and analytical method of thought. It necessitates deliberate effort, concentrated attention, and logical reasoning. System two thinking requires cognitive resources and is employed for complicated issue solving and careful decision-making. It moves more slowly and deliberately than system one.

Fear is one of the first emotions we may experience at the start of a crisis. It can lead to rash actions, unfavourable outcomes, and a deterioration in capacity to think effectively and creatively. Fear influences how we manage relationships, prioritize work, and make educated decisions. When President Franklin Delano Roosevelt famously said, "Only thing we have to fear is fear itself,"[11] he was not just bringing forward a catchy phrase to attract support for his programs. He was speaking to a nation in the grip of what would become known as the Great Depression. His statement, however, is not correct, as there are many other things to be afraid of, such as sharks, taxes, and worldwide pandemics. Because fear can drive poor decision-making, it can result in the negative outcomes we want to avoid. While there are many things to fear, one of the most harmful is fear itself.

While it can be challenging to do so, leaders at all levels of organizations need to understand how they manage fear and practice overcoming it. They can prepare by practising mental self-control, self-regulation, and the ability to assess disruptive mental patterns or moods. One approach is to become more aware of the three "selves" that influence our behaviour in times of danger and threat: ME, US, and THEM.

---

11   "'Only Thing We Have to Fear Is Fear Itself': FDR's First Inaugural Address," History Matters, accessed October 31, 2023, https://historymatters.gmu.edu/d/5057/.

"ME" and My Compass in a Crisis

Similar to my world of sailing, I like to think of a crisis as a compass. I consider myself the centre, or *"ME,"* in this crisis compass, as a compass has a centre and four directions. East and West signify communication within *"US,"* which refers to the team, organization, and internal resources. Meanwhile, north, and south signify searching outside of us, or *"THEM,"* to identify opportunities that require the use of external resources at all levels.

When navigating the unfamiliar waters of a crisis, three crucial pillars must be considered. The initial pillar: "Know Myself First," as I am the centre of this compass. I must recognize my own limitations and work to develop leadership skills. Although some people may have hereditary features that incline them toward leadership, these are not required to be effective leaders. The second pillar is "Know Us" (the east and west directions). This entails evaluating the objective truth of the current situation in collaboration with my team, associates, and other internal resources. During a crisis, we must be brutally honest with ourselves and analyze everyone's skills and shortcomings because not everyone can oversee the same amount of urgency. The third and final pillar is "Know Them," which refers to the north and south directions. This entails evaluating our internal and external relationships as well as our available resources. It is critical to inventory our resources and prioritize their use both during and after the crisis. We can obtain resources both internally and externally through our interactions and connections. This includes those to whom we report, as well as individuals and organizations in our society, government agencies, and even the media.

Navigating a crisis is an up-and-down exercise, which means we may need to reach out to people in various levels of our business as well as those in our external network. We may design a course forward and effectively navigate uncharted waters by employing this compass analogy and focusing on the three pillars of crisis negotiation.

"ME" Being a Rational Leader during a Crisis

Scholars have long disputed whether leaders are born or made. The 1841 great man theory of Thomas Carlyle[12] stated that leaders were born with leadership traits, which encouraged studies of inheritable attributes. The attribute theory of leadership outlines personality traits and characteristics that are associated with successful leadership in a variety of contexts.

However, psychologists such as Ralph Melvin Stogdill claimed that leadership was established by an individual's engagement with the social context rather than by predetermined features.

Early research also looked at characteristics between leaders and followers and discovered that leaders were better communicators, more extroverted, more self-assured, and taller, but these differences were minor.[13] Without a doubt, an individual's background and experiences will have an impact on their leadership qualities.

In their book *The Leadership Challenge*, initially published in 1987, James M. Kouzes and Barry Z. Posner stated that "believability is an important leadership quality."[14] They recognized three crucial components of a leader's credibility: honesty, inspiration, and competency. Possessing

---

12   "Great Man Theory and Trait Theory of Leadership," Your Article Library, accessed October 31, 2023, https://www.yourarticlelibrary.com/leadership/great-man-theory-and-trait-theory-of-leadership/28004.

13   Mark Travers, "New Research Challenges the Notion that Extroverts Are Naturally Better in Leadership Positions," Forbes, March 18, 2022, https://www.forbes.com/sites/traversmark/2022/03/18/new-research-challenges-the-notion-that-extroverts-are-naturally-better-in-leadership-positions/.

14   Melvin U. Damaolao, "Book Review: The Leadership Challenge by James M. Kouzes and Barry Z. Posner," International Journal of Research Studies in Education 11, no. 4 (February 13, 2022): 77–81, https://consortiacademia.org/wp-content/uploads/2020/v11i04/22153_ijrse_final.pdf.

the majority of a leader's characteristics does not guarantee that one will become an effective leader. Only a few leaders possess all or most of the characteristics of effective leadership; however, it is debatable if some people can never become leaders. Everyone has the capacity to become a powerful leader, but it is akin to discovering a treasure at the bottom of the sea, which has little to no worth until it is brought to the surface.

The most significant characteristics during a crisis are determined by how the situation develops and how leaders and the group interpret urgencies. The combination of these attributes and the issue at hand influences leadership quality. It is not, however, proper to judge leadership simply amid a crisis. Leaders who have successfully navigated a crisis or have been "battle tested" are stronger leaders. A crisis has an impact on the person, the organization, and the resources used to manage the problem. To be successful, people must manage their three selves, connect their beliefs with their capacities, and bring their treasures to the surface while facing the challenges that come with them. They must deal with important situations that are fraught with uncertainty.

They must negotiate unfamiliar territory and comprehend the implications for all parties involved. They must decide on a plan of action and recognize that the results will affect everyone. As new channels for leadership emerge, such as social media and e-commerce, the characteristics required for success evolve. In this arena, the ability to influence is more significant than the ability to lead.

Natural disasters have many unexpected components when compared to other types of crises. When confronting such crisis, we have the impression that powers beyond our comprehension are at stake, daring us to fail if we do not accept the call to lead ourselves, our team, and others.

Curtain Is up on "ME"!

Growing up in a culturally vibrant atmosphere in Casablanca exposed me to live theatre on a regular basis. My city's expat community valued our diverse cultures, and seeing plays with live performers was always an exciting experience for me. Theatre actors must be faultless on stage, with no tolerance for error, and their talent astounded me. The opportunities to "take two" as in movie productions is not a customary practice when performing live on stage.

I was always excited when I heard the unmistakable knocks that signalled the start of a performance, and the lights went down. The thrill of seeing life interpreted live on stage was breathtaking. Years later, in Fort McMurray, I found myself in a situation that forced me to perform like a stage actor. I realized I would be watched and listened to, and my actions would be scrutinized on how I would oversee the situation and control my emotions. I sure couldn't afford to forget my lines. My previous traumatic sea experiences had a tremendous impact on my mental "script," which assisted me in navigating the situation I was about to encounter.

Shortly after the curtain goes up, a play will lay out the framework of the story through various scenes in the beginning. This framework or structure guides the story's progression, such as acts, scenes, or plot points. The actors lay out their roles and relationships as the audience grasps the plot.

There are some parallels between seeing a play and dealing with a crisis. The plot of the story unfolds with numerous lines and scenarios throughout a crisis. A crisis also necessitates a framework or plan outlining the processes and actions required to address it. Individuals and organizations must be able to manage unexpected events and make swift decisions during a crisis, much as performers must react and adapt to changes in a play. Both necessitate strategy and preparedness.

To ensure a smooth presentation, actors and crew must rehearse their lines and motions in a play. Actors play distinctive characters with distinct personalities, motivations, and behaviours. Individuals or organizations must take on certain roles and responsibilities during a crisis to responsibly manage the situation. Leaders must have strategies in place and practice exercises to ensure they are ready to respond successfully in an emergency.

If a prop fails or a line is lost during a performance, players must be able to respond swiftly and adjust to the unexpected scenario. Leaders must also be able to adapt to changing situations and make swift judgments based on the facts at their disposal.

Both demand clear communication. Actors in a play must communicate successfully with one another and with the audience to convey the story and emotions. Leaders must communicate effectively with their team, stakeholders, and the public during a crisis to deliver updates, instructions, and comfort.

Finally, both can be emotionally difficult. To create a believable portrayal in a play, actors may need to delve into profound emotions. In a crisis, leaders must manage their own emotions while also supporting their team and stakeholders who may be experiencing dread, worry, or grief. Both require similar talents and characteristics in general, such as planning, adaptability, effective communication, and emotional intelligence.

In the excellent book on crisis leadership, *You're It,* authors Leonard J. Marcus, Eric J. McNulty, Joseph M. Henderson, and Barry C. Dorn highlight that as a leader, "You're it." "You are responsible for more than just yourself. People are counting on you, from your subordinates to your boss, from your peers and your collaborators to your customers, your suppliers, and even the public."[15]

---

15   Leonard J. Marcus, Eric J. McNulty, Joseph M. Henderson, and Barry C. Dorn, You're It: Crisis, Change, and How to Lead When It Matters Most (New York: Hachette Book Group, 2021), 22–23.

"ME," Managing the Crisis; the Crisis Does Not Manage "ME"!

Personal Log: Fort McMurray, Alberta, May 3, 2016, 2:30 to 3:30 p.m.: Through Hell!

I drove with a wall of flames on my left and felt the intense heat in front of me. I made my way downtown to the Clearwater Suite Hotel, my main hotel headquarters. But my priority was to check on my wife, Donna, whose office was on the northern side of town. She was then the property manager responsible for overseeing twenty-three hundred condominium units in Fort McMurray. The local radio stations were already broadcasting mandatory evacuation orders for various parts of the town, and Donna informed me that her head office had asked her to pack important documents and secure the computers. She saw flames close to her office, as the fire had jumped the Athabasca River by then.

Meanwhile, I had a conference call scheduled with my general managers for 3:00 p.m. Upon arrival at the Clearwater Suite Hotel, I sensed the team was extremely nervous. My immediate task was to follow protocol and evacuate all guests while securing the property as best we could. During the call with the managers, I instructed them to be prepared to evacuate their respective properties and to keep a record of rooms that were not checked out. Most of our guests were working on oil sand sites 20 to 40 km from downtown and were not likely to return to retrieve their belongings. I advised the managers to send their teams to join their families, secure all exits and in-house guest records, take the cash on hand, and lock the property.

I further instructed everyone to email their personal contacts to my second-in-command, Mike, who would centralize communications between us all in the next few hours via our hotel's Facebook group. I asked Mike to broadcast a message such as, "Once you are reunited with your family, get the hell out of Dodge." Fort McMurray has only one main road, Highway 63, so I advised them to head toward Edmonton, 450 km south; however, if the main road was closed because of the fire's unpredictable nature, they should go north. The local radio stations were broadcasting the same message.

I asked one unmarried volunteer to stay while I rushed home. While driving home, I saw a massive wall of flame and an orange glare in the inky sky all around me. I called my wife, who was calmly packing, and told her to join me back downtown as soon as possible, confirming that I would pick up our puppy, Baby Jaxx, as well as our passports and other essentials.

Driving back downtown, I noticed that all the gas stations were out of gas, and I realized I had forgotten all our medicines. Despite this, I made sure my puppy had a blanket and his favourite toys, as the amygdala in my brain played different tricks with my priorities during these initial times of crisis. My immediate priorities were that my wife, team, and I would be safe and come out alive.

Highway 63 was congested on both sides, but I drove against traffic heading downtown to my office at the Clearwater Suite Hotel. Cars and trucks lined up the roads, but everyone departed in an orderly fashion.

On my way, I received a series of calls from representatives of our ownership and management company, Atlific, asking me for the status of the situation. I reported to CEO Robert Chartrand that we were on mandatory evacuation and would keep him informed as best as I could in the next few hours. My priorities were to focus on my family first, the team second, and the assets third, which included eight properties localized in the south, downtown, and north of town. Some of the first thoughts I had were: What is required of me? How can I best ensure that I use all the expertise, resources, and team I need to get us out of this mess alive?

Leading amid a crisis necessitates the use of existing leadership practices while coping with the situation's complexities. You do not have a script to follow, and you need to decide swiftly while dealing with many minor problems at the same time. It is critical to recognize that a leader controls the crisis rather than the other way around. This mindset is essential for being focused and level-headed. Perfection is difficult, if not impossible, to accomplish. Too many variables are beyond your control, and the situation is continuously changing. It is critical to avoid getting bogged down in the details and to keep your eyes on the larger picture. Otherwise, you will be managed by the crisis.

During an interview with Michael Lewis for *Vanity Fair*, President Obama stated: "Nothing comes to my desk that is perfectly solvable. Otherwise, someone else would have solved it."[16] Instead, he dealt with probability and chose acceptable results over optimal ones.

While leaders play a significant role in resolving a crisis, the resources and overall support they receive are also crucial factors in their success. Leadership is defined by actions and attitude rather than rank or position. To responsibly manage a crisis, a leader must possess key competencies. They must be confident in managing their emotions and anxieties when under inspection. Because of internal and external forces, the leader must respond with the same competencies as in regular situations. People must trust and respect you to be a great leader, and creating this trust and confidence inside the organization is critical. Your followers must comprehend and accept your beliefs; they must believe in your mission.

Poor leadership can cause an organization to crumble quickly. The acclaimed leadership expert John C. Maxwell reminds us in his book *The 21 Irrefutable Laws of Leadership* that leadership is a choice based on one's

---

16   "Barack Obama to Michael Lewis on a Presidential Loss of Freedom: 'You Don't Get Used to It—At Least, I Don't,'" Vanity Fair, September 5, 2012, https://www.vanityfair.com/news/2012/09/barack-obama-michael-lewis.

values. Before you can lead others, you must first lead yourself. This neces-sitates answering some critical questions about yourself, such as who you are, what inspires you, and what your values are. You must ask yourself why others should follow you and what makes you a worthy leader to follow.

You must align your team's priorities, identities, and personalities toward a common purpose. A good leader sets a good example. They must address obstacles head-on and be able to rally their team around a single goal. While leadership qualities are crucial in any situation, they are especially important in times of crisis. Financial remuneration does not motivate leaders at a certain level of seniority; rather, they strive for a challenge that will motivate them. Some, like me, prefer challenges that are more complex.

You will frequently have to reconcile the organization's and team's priorities with your own personal priorities. The fundamental instinct is to protect one's family first. This was evident for myself, my team, and all residents during the wildfires and flood in Fort McMurray. A student's letter stated how they were enjoying a movie when a teacher came in and shuttered all the windows. Outside, the sky was black and purple, and the grass looked ashy. Parents and staff were summoned to pick up their ter-rified children. A mother recalled the anguish of leaving her house and possessions behind, only to realize that her family's safety was all that mattered. Amid a crisis, protecting one's family is a primal instinct, and leaders must recognize this and ensure that their team is likewise protected and supported.

Personal Log: Fort McMurray, Alberta, May 3, 2016, 5:30 p.m.: Through Hell!

I stayed downtown in Fort McMurray, where two employees from our housekeeping department waited for their family to join them so they could evacuate. I directed Mike and Colleen Humphrey, our revenue manager for the region based in Calgary, to coordi-nate all available hotel rooms within our other properties managed by Atlific in Alberta, with suites that had kitchens for those with families. Colleen had direct access to live room inventory and could assign evacuees. I instructed Mike to use our Facebook group as the primary means of communication for all team members to receive information.

We also made ad hoc group calls with our general managers in the coming hours as the situation developed. Sadly, Mike informed me he lost his house, but thankfully, his family and pets were safe. I also learned that one of my other general managers, Alona, was forced to stand in a small river for safety and watch as her house burned to the ground. She was waiting for her husband, who was at the oil sands site, to pick her up.

By this time, local radio stations had stopped broadcasting and people had vacated the broadcast studios. I called my wife regularly. She was finishing clearing her office and was on her way to meet me. She confirmed that the flames were getting dangerously close to the townhouses where we lived. I urged her to hurry, as the situation was quickly spiralling out of control. Around 5:00 p.m., I received a call from my catering director, who was stuck on the highway by the airport and asked me to save his two dogs stuck inside his downtown condominium near our hotel. I asked one of the two team members left waiting for their families to join them to come with me.

We drove through a deserted town with just a few cars on the roads and local police monitoring various crossroads. The air was thick with smoke, and we could see flames above the Abasand residential hill, close to our hotel. Unfortunately, we could not open the door and free the two dogs inside. I could hear cars and propane tanks exploding from houses across the hill where the fire was raging, and my stomach tightened as a sense of desperation set in.

We left with heavy hearts, unable to save the dogs but hoping someone could rescue them later (they did). Helicopters buzzed overhead as we drove back to the hotel. The major streets and stores were deserted. Dogs walked the streets, having escaped via low-level patios.

I felt powerless, but I quickly mentally regrouped.

The synchronization of the lights and the players on stage can enhance the spectator experience of any performance. Your actions in times of crisis will put you in the spotlight and expose who you are.

Because the environment is always changing, it is critical to make decisions rapidly rather than precisely. In my own journey as a leader, I have come to truly value the art of swiftly dissecting information, homing in on its core, and then forging ahead with unwavering decisions. It is like peering through a whirlwind of details to uncover the significant part.

Yet, I have also had my share of encounters with the specter of cognitive overload. It can sneak in when information is scarce, when conflicting interests tug at your thoughts and when emotions are running high. The result? A sort of mental paralysis that can stymie even the most analytical minds, especially when your part of a complex web of decision-makers is striving for consensus.

So, what is the antidote to this inertia? I have found that it takes a conscious effort to break free from the chains that hold you back. It is about zeroing in on the pivotal aspects that uphold the continuity of your business, all the while nurturing the potential for enduring success.

In the realm of rapid decision-making, I have discovered the power of a streamlined framework. It is like having a reliable compass amid chaos. Equally important, though, is the art of discerning what not to do. During the tumult of a crisis, the spotlight naturally falls on the tasks that demand immediate attention. But it is equally crucial to recognize what can wait—a strategic choreography of priorities.

In my experience, crisis management extends beyond just doing what is urgent. It involves identifying those vital few priorities that must take precedence. Think of it as shaping the initial stages of a crisis by framing the essentials: safeguarding employees, ensuring financial resilience, maintaining top-notch customer service, and securing operational flow.

One lesson I have learned is the significance of meticulous documentation. It is like anchoring your decisions in written clarity, ensuring that everyone is on the same page. Flexibility, of course, remains key, as you steer your course based on unfolding events. In the grand scheme of leadership, this approach has become a cornerstone for me. It is a testament to the delicate balance between seizing opportunities and orchestrating a complex stage "play" navigating through strategic restraint.

As the financial urgencies surge in the immediacy of the crisis, large initiatives and expenses should be postponed, and prioritization should be strict and disciplined. We should advertise the "what not to do" options through the ranks. Because conflicts may occur between defined priorities or between the urgent and the important, smart trade-offs are required. It is critical to place decision-makers in the central command "war room" and to empower the front lines to make decisions where practicable. Leaders should also reinforce or create direct ties at all levels of the business, as well as set systems for knowledge to quickly cascade to the front line. Early and frequent situational evaluations are required, and local leaders and influencers should be brought together to share knowledge about the crisis's impact and stakeholder feelings.

It is critical to embrace action, and leaders should not punish mistakes because they are unavoidable. It is better to act than not act. Bold adaptability is essential, and leaders must anticipate shifting conditions. Seeking input and information from a variety of sources, admitting what is unknown, and bringing in outside experts when needed can assist leaders in making swift adjustments and developing new plans of attack.

From my own leadership journey, I have come to recognize the essence of casting one's antennae everywhere across the diverse landscapes of operation. As a leader, it is akin to extending your senses, like tendrils, into every corner of the ecosystems you navigate. We will cover this important topic later in this book.

Melissa Blake, Mayor of Wood Buffalo, recalls the day that forever impacted her community:

> I went to a morning meeting, then to the daily update, which announced the state of local emergency on Sunday night. As I watched the fire spread from the seventh floor, my fear grew. Watching the traffic pour down Abasand late in the afternoon was terrible, but we could not evacuate everyone and had to delay those leaving the critical regions even more, so I wanted to tell everyone else to pack their bags but not to worry. I considered how to preserve communication between emergency and

public operations. There was no plan or anticipation of a full evacuation; the emphasis was clearly on containing the footprint of the existing fires.[17]

During a crisis, unpredictable situations will develop, and, like a roller coaster ride, emotions and stomach tightness will surface; however, a calm mind will carry leaders and their teams ahead. Sharp curves, bumps, and difficulties await, and it is critical to react courageously and act while prioritizing what is most important.

"ME" Delivering Results

Along my leadership path, I have often heard the adage, "There are two kinds of leaders: those who bring you excuses and those who bring you results." Very few of the former will ever deliver on the latter.

What I have discovered on my own leadership journey is the significance of personally shouldering responsibility. It is an acknowledgment that challenges often sprawl beyond our immediate control. In these times, my approach has been to weave a sense of unity within my team, refocusing our collective energies, and fostering a culture of accountability.

A daily ritual that has proven invaluable for me is always crafting a dashboard of priorities, like a map guiding us through the tumultuous seas of crisis. It helped discipline my mind. Distilling these priorities onto half a page, no more, helps crystallized my focus. What is equally crucial is ensuring consensus among those who tread this path alongside me.

Amid the crisis, I have also come to realize the power of constant assessment. Regular check-ins help harmonized our efforts. It is during these moments that I set the stage with key performance indicators and metrics, choosing a select few that encapsulate our week's aspirations. This act of judicious selection acknowledges the inevitable influx of fresh challenges and urgent demands.

Yet, even as the storm rages, the helm of leadership demands personal upkeep. For me, it had become a ritual of self-care, a regimen that nourishes

---

17   June Warren, "Saving Wood Buffalo," JWN and Westbrier Communications Inc., 2016, 22.

both mind and body—a combination of a wholesome diet, invigorating exercise, and moments of reflections.

At the core of this mayhem, however, is the team. They are the heartbeats of our endeavours. It is a delicate balance of empathy and understanding their unique circumstances, while also igniting their motivation through clear, transparent communication. The connection between leaders and their teams is vital. A top-to-bottom flow of communication bridges gaps and clears the path forward. Recognizing the power of collaboration, I have learned to identify the strengths within the team, delegating specific tasks crucial for our survival.

Yet, our survival is not solely within our own walls. Outreach to customers and suppliers become a lifeline, executed with caution and empathy. Crisis will have a significant impact on any cash flows—yours and theirs. Continuous and timely updates as the crisis develops and stabilizes will help build relationship and trust.

As events unfold quickly, it is essential to understand the most critical information necessary for action to avoid feeling overwhelmed. You do not want to appear irrational and must not allow yourself to be perceived as indecisive.

To navigate the crisis successfully, you must first understand yourself and how you work with others. As the crisis unfolds quickly, you need to have a sense of the "big picture" and the potential impact your decisions could have on everyone involved. You will need to dig into the details while maintaining a broader perspective to make informed decisions. Maintaining focus and considering the consequences of your decisions are essential. By doing so, you will be able to act quickly and decisively without sacrificing the quality of your decision-making.

Regardless of your purpose, celebrate your daily heroes who made it possible, especially if their efforts go unnoticed.

"ME" Using Skills and Knowledge during a Crisis

During a stressful situation, I was asked if skills were more important than knowledge and which of the two was better suited to act under pressure. Knowledge refers to being familiar with information and theoretical concepts, which can be shared among individuals or attained through personal observation and study. Understanding the issue, its causes, and potential solutions requires knowledge of the relevant laws, regulations, and protocols connected to the crisis; without this knowledge, it is difficult to make educated decisions and act.

Skill represents the capacity to effectively apply one's knowledge within unique contexts. In my journey of professional growth, I nurtured these skills through a blend of ongoing observation, continuous learning, and attentive engagement with the experiences and wisdom—or not—of those around me. Along the way, as I ascended the corporate ladder, I learned more about what not to do than what to do. It is through trial and error that I discovered the most successful path to attaining proficiency in various skills.

I have often found myself equipped with knowledge, but it is in the act of applying that knowledge that its true value shines. It is like having a toolbox filled with tools: you might have all the right instruments, but unless you know how to employ them effectively, they remain dormant.

On the other side, honing a skill is like sharpening a blade. You might become an expert at using a particular tool, but if you are unsure of when, where, and how to use it, its potential remains untapped. It is in the fusion of skill and application that true mastery emerges.

Learning leadership along my personal journey, I have discovered that it is not just about possessing knowledge or mastering a skill; it is about the intricate balance between the two. It is about marrying the "what" with the "how," creating a constructive collaboration that transforms mere potential into impactful action.

Decision-making skills and sustainability skills are key abilities to have when facing a crisis. With decision-making skills, you must understand the situation as best as you can in a short amount of time. Your focus should be on gathering all the facts, analyzing the data, developing solutions, comparing options, and finally selecting the best course of action. This works well in normal situations, but in a crisis, it is necessary to adapt and decide quickly. Research by military strategist John Boyd and other business strategists has shown that situational awareness is more important in crisis situations. Later on, I will emphasize how military discipline and systems are excellent tools to use in times of crisis.

It is critical to have sustainability skills in times of crisis to effectively manage the situation. Here are some sustainability skills that can help:

Team formation. This is the capacity to quickly construct teams led by competent individuals to connect departments or organizations on the scene and link them to a main operation centre. In my experience, having an operating picture goes beyond just seeing what is in front of you. It is like having a mental map that not only highlights immediate situations but also assesses potential risks and opportunities. It is about being attuned to the dynamic environment, where all opportunities are looked at.

Networking takes this awareness to a new level. It is like weaving a web that connects you to a diverse array of individuals and sources, whether they are right there with you or far beyond the scene. These connections become a treasure trove of wisdom, gathered from different experiences and perspectives. It is about tapping into this wealth of knowledge to shape a more complete view of the situation. We will cover later in this book how networking plays a most significant role in times of crisis and recovery.

Fluidity. I have also found that effective leadership demands a certain level of fluidity. It is like adapting the structure to the situation at hand, streamlining communication and decision-making across multiple departments. Under this lean yet interconnected framework, common goals become the guiding light and action plans emerge through collaborative constructive interaction. The crux of it all lies in the ability to channel personal efforts within a unified structure. It is like orchestrating a symphony, where every instrument plays its part to achieve a harmonious outcome. This unity within diversity becomes the link for taking control of crises, steering them towards resolution.

Communication. In a crisis, communication is the ability to receive and transmit voice, video, and data into real time. The capacity to separate the "noise" from the "reality" coming from many sources is critical. Being able to listen with a focus on selecting the most relevant information for the benefit of all is essential to achieving a successful outcome. I will further elaborate in this book on how communication, coordination, and collaboration all play a vital role in a crisis.

"ME" Leading the Crisis

Personal Log: Fort McMurray, Alberta, May 3, 2016, 5:30 p.m. to 8:00 p.m.: Through Hell!

After conversing with Mike, who monitored our Facebook page traffic, I felt more confident. We reached most of our team members. Colleen, our regional revenue manager, was busy preparing a map for the evacuees, showing the properties they, along with their families and pets, would be assigned to stay in. We had properties in several locations, including Edmonton, Red Deer, Calgary, Lloydminster, and Lake Louise.

At the time of the evacuation, we had 157 active employees, all of whom had families and pets. I requested that Mike record all needs and work with Colleen to accommodate everyone as efficiently as possible. A few team members headed south towards the cities, while some went north towards the oil sand sites, where they could seek temporary refuge in the "camps." These camps are comprised of well-built trailers with all the amenities one would expect from regular accommodations, including food facilities, gyms, and auxiliary services that could cater to over six thousand workers. While I hoped the wildfires would not reach them, I could not shake the worry in the back of my mind, as fire and oil do not mix well.

As I scrolled through my phone, I came across rumours that the Radisson, our south property, was burning and that the Vantage suites on the highway were also being ravaged. A competitor, the Super 8, had already been destroyed by then. I had to redirect my focus, however, towards our immediate situation and felt relieved to know that a communication process was in place and our evacuation plan was being executed. I immediately contacted the owners and VP of our management company, Robert Chartrand, and gave them a quick update on our status and company hotel assets.

For the time being, our team was heading towards various shelters in our region, but I could not confirm the status of the properties until I physically inspected them at a later point, depending on how events would unfold. Most of us were not fully aware of the extent of the damage caused in certain parts of the town, forcing some of us into a long exile out of Fort McMurray.

Later, I received a call from a French national CBC radio station inquiring about our situation. I described it as precarious, and although, we had experienced no loss of life within our group so far, I politely asked them to contact me again early tomorrow morning when I would have a better idea of our situation. The last thing I wanted was to add unconfirmed rumours to the already overwhelming number of truths, rumours, and facts being broadcasted through various mediums.

Starting from the bottom in the "basement" is not wrong as a crisis leader but refrain from making major life decisions while on that lower floor and avoid giving important speeches or statements until you get a handle on the situation. Visit "other floors" and think of ways to get yourself and your team out of the crisis. You may not have all the solutions, and your survival instinct may limit your options, but it is critical to engage in rational thinking.

Remember that in extreme events, leadership is the art of encouraging others to adapt to the novelty by leaping to a network command and control system that can connect, communicate, and coordinate to produce public value. Resist the desire to panic and act quickly; instead, utilize the opening minutes of the crisis to organize questions and prioritize the importance of the situation, establish communication, and assemble an initial emergency team with rational strategies.

We all remember the dramatic moments on September 11, 2001, when former US President George W. Bush was informed by his chief of staff while helping young students reading the "Pet Goat" that the World Trade Center had been hit by planes. No one knew the enormity of the loss of life that would follow. To avoid alarming the children and adults in the room, President Bush waited in the classroom after the immediate shock had gone. His mind was clearly rushing towards panic, but he maintained a stern and resolved demeanour.[18]

Making sense of what is happening at the start of a crisis can be difficult since many minor events are intertwined with the main event. To acquire an initial grasp of the crisis, use the basic Five W's: what, when, which, who, and where.

- *What* exactly happened?

- *When* did it occur?

- *Which* priority needs my immediate attention?

- *Who* has been harmed?

- *Where* should I first focus myself and team on?

How it happened and who is to blame may not be an immediate necessity to know, but they should be on the outskirts of your mind so you can change accordingly. As you are getting acclimated to this new emergency environment, I recommend the following skills to learn:

Learn to assess. Acting rapidly may give you erroneous perceptions, and you may offer immediate directives that must be changed on short notice, causing confusion within the ranks.

Learn to interpret. You will receive a massive amount of data or information that may contradict your initial beliefs on your instant response to the crisis; constantly absorb, digest, read, and listen to a variety of sources.

Learn to empower. Ensure that everyone feels comfortable addressing issues in the spirit of cooperation and ultimate respect, and delegate jobs and responsibilities to your closest associates.

---

18   Asfin Yurdakul, "He Told Bush That 'America Is under Attack,'" NBC News, September 10, 2009, https://www.nbcnews.com/id/wbna32782623

Learn to ask the right questions. Avoid thinking you have all the answers and stay focused on the facts you must have right now.

Learn to delegate. Delegate as many operational chores as possible while still giving time for contemplation for you and your immediate leadership team.

Learn to prioritize. Create checklists at all levels, including your own. Stress and tension can make it difficult to concentrate, and a checklist will return you to a more disciplined mindset.

Learn to adapt and be flexible. While checklists are an amazing technique, they will not provide you with all the solutions required; use them to challenge yourself with possibilities along the road.

Learn clarity as your best asset. Know as much as you can about who is doing what, where, when, and why.

Learn to obtain control. People will look and listen to you for comfort. Avoid using too many loud directions. Show firmness and resolve without engaging in fights. When rushing to the summit, remember that your mental ability has a limit; learn to take a "breather."

Learn to say, "Not now!" If the media inquires about your status, give a brief overview with a limited commitment on your part, and politely and respectfully request a more appropriate time when you will have more information to share with the public.

Personal Log: Fort McMurray, Alberta, May 3, 2016, 6:30 p.m. to 8:30 p.m.: Through Hell!

I attempted to call Donna but could not reach her. Worry gnawed at me until we finally connected, and she informed me she and one of her assistants were trapped in traffic with flames fast approaching their car. Panic set in, and I asked if I should join her, but she confirmed that all roads leading to the main highways were packed with evacuees. We agreed to hope for the best and be together soon. I realized the necessity of a phone charger in times of crisis and collected a few, just in case.

As I stepped out of the property, I heard the continuous explosions of trucks and gas tanks from Abasand Hill, across our property, with flames rapidly approaching. I quickly contacted our regional sales manager in Calgary, seeking help from his industry contacts to secure space in our properties and that of other competitors and universities in case we needed additional space. At 7:00 p.m., the families of my last two employees joined them, and finally, Donna entered the property, providing much-needed relief.

She recounted the horrors she had witnessed as flames licked her car. Thankfully, one of the first water bombers covered her area with floods of water, and she was later driven by a police officer to our property, leaving her car where it was.

We regrouped and left shortly, driving to Anzac, a community located around 30 km south of Fort McMurray, where an initial evacuation post was hastily erected for displaced citizens.

At that moment, I thought it would be the most suitable place to weather the last dramatic hours we all sustained while being confident that we would be back in a day or two, unaware of how severe the situation was going to get. I did a final round of the property and noticed an eerie silence as no more cars or trucks were present on the highway. I shivered at the sight of flames across the highway from my property and the incessant booms of cars and houses exploding high across from us on the Abasand residential hill. I unplugged as many machines and computers as I could lay my hands on, ensured that all offices doors were unlocked to allow free access to fire fighters intervention, and gave a quick call to our owners and Robert, confirming that I was the last one leaving and would communicate my whereabouts in a few hours.

I still did not know the magnitude of the wildfires and had some internal concerns about the safety of the roads out of town. My plan B was to head closer to one of the three rivers surrounding our town if the fires trapped us in town. If the situation worsened, we would jump into it, hoping our puppy, Jaxx, would learn to swim rather quickly.

After contacting everyone and finding that they were safe and evacuated and that all our buildings were locked up with no guests left, I shuttered the property at 8:30 p.m. and drove away with Donna and Jaxx. The town had a feeling of total abandonment as we joined the last of our fellow citizens and evacuees on our pilgrimage to find a safe harbour and stay alive.

I felt like something had been stolen from us, and I was powerless to do anything about it. I was frustrated by the sudden rush of events while seeing flames and smoke all around us. Embers were dropping on top of my car, but I kept myself calm and collected for the benefit of our own health and safety.

"ME" and Learning My Priorities

In challenging situations in the past, I made a conscious effort to maintain a calm and composed demeanour, recognizing that our well-being hinged on it. This was a deeply personal commitment, an act of safeguarding our health and safety.

Reflecting on my own journey, I have come to understand the profound significance of discovering my priorities. It is like a journey inward, uncovering the core elements that truly matter in my life.

In the nineteenth century, the Prussian military theorist Carl von Clausewitz wrote the first scholarly study on military strategy.[19] In his work, he identified three essential elements of commanding. The first is the ability of great commanders, such as Napoleon Bonaparte, to recognize how to win a battle in a single "glance" during their pre-battle evaluation. Clausewitz uses the French expression *"coup d'oeil." Coup d'oeil* is about swiftly grasping truths that might remain hidden to ordinary minds. It is a skill that requires rapid insight, a glimpse into possibilities, and a quick assessment of consequences before charting a course of action.

---

19 Lennart Souchon, "Strategy, War, and the Relevance of Carl von Clausewitz," Military Strategy Magazine, Special Edition, "The Continuing Relevance of Clausewitz," December 2020, 33–37, https://www.militarystrategymagazine.com/article/strategy-war-and-the-relevance-of-carl-von-clausewitz/.

Clausewitz did not stop there. He unveiled the importance of resolute decision-making and unwavering commitment, even amid uncertainty. This resonates deeply with my personal ethos—the resolve to stand firm in the face of doubt and forge ahead with my choices, trusting in their validity.

The concept of "presence of mind" struck a chord within me. It is the art of maintaining flexibility, the ability to adapt and respond to the unexpected without faltering. In many ways, it is an embodiment of the agility I have come to value in my own life.

This notion found a modern parallel through the work of psychologist Gary Klein, who meticulously studied decision-making in high-pressure scenarios. Through his research on firefighters, emergency-room nurses, and combat soldiers, Klein unveiled a truth that reverberates in my own experiences. He advised leaders not to become fixated on their initial strategy and to embrace the fact that they will have to alter their route as time passes and conditions change.

Klein said,

Rather than seeing people lock in and commit so that they can reduce all the anxiety they feel about making the decision. They should say, *'There's a good chance I'm going to have to adapt, I'm going to have to modify my plan and even my goals.* I want to be on the lookout for counter-indicators. If people have some different ideas than the ones that I'm holding, I don't want them to mess up my momentum, but I don't want to silence them either. I want to make sure that they're still gathering evidence for their point-of-view. Then they can bring me that evidence as it arises, so that I'm not blinkered, I am not just proceeding on blindly.[20]

In my personal readings, I have discovered a trough of insights from these scholars, each resonating with my own journey. From the swift discernment of truth to the unwavering determination in decision-making

---

20   Bruce Hoffman, "Top Decision-Making Expert Says Leaders Need to Get Comfortable with Uncertainty. " Forbes, July,17,2021, https://forbes.com/sites/ brycehoffman/2021/07/17/ top-decision-making-expert-says-leaders-need-to-get-comfortable-with-incertainty/?sh=46ac6obed4b2f

and the fifth sense of adaptability amid uncertainty, these concepts have become guiding lights in my pursuit of purpose and meaning.

People, however, focus on the person or task in front of them rather than the ground or background on which the person or task stands. During times of disaster, leaders go through three separate, interrelated stages: Where does pain come from? How can we contain it? How can we overcome the original negativity? After accepting current conditions, they also ask themselves: How do I capture what's essential, learn from it, and maintain constant beneficial interrelationships with each other? What comes next? How do I rally everyone around a shared goal to execute?

There have been numerous occasions in the past where critical information or difficulties were not identified immediately during a crisis or pre-crisis, resulting in such adverse effects that people have lost their lives. A few examples I can recollect verifying this fact are:

Hurricane Katrina. In 2005, Hurricane Katrina devastated the Gulf Coast of the United States. A critical error that arose during this crisis was the delayed reaction exhibited by government authorities regarding the gravity of the storm and the subsequent inundation it brought about. Essential pieces of information, including the possibility of levee failure, were not effectively disseminated. This lack of proper communication led to a sluggish and insufficient response, resulting in the loss of numerous lives and incurring billions of dollars in damages.

Deepwater Horizon oil spill. An explosion on the Deepwater Horizon oil rig in 2010, in the Gulf of Mexico, resulted in the greatest marine oil spill in history. A major mistake made during this crisis was to ignore the potential environmental effects of the spill. At first, they assumed that the oil spill was minor and minimized its impact on the environment, resulting in inadequate response measures that caused significant ecological harm and had long-term consequences for sea creatures and the region's economy.

The Fukushima Daiichi disaster. This disaster occurred in 2011 at the Fukushima Daiichi nuclear power plant in Japan, causing considerable damage to the nuclear power plant. One of the significant mistakes made during this crisis was a lack of preparedness for a nuclear disaster. Crucial details, such as the risks associated with the plant's design and location, were not adequately communicated, leading to a slow and inadequate response.

The Lahaina fires devastation. Maui surviving residents were extremely concerned and critical whether more could have been done to alert them. Sirens stationed around the island intended to warn of impending disasters never sounded. The local emergencies authorities chose social media not only realizing a lot of their panicked citizens were not in possession of phones, but widespread power and cellular outages hampered other forms of alerting. Witnesses said they had little warnings if any. As Lahaina was engulfed in a storm of embers and sparks, some desperate people dove into the Pacific Ocean to escape.

It is most critical to quickly identify and prioritize critical issues during a crisis and effectively communicate them to the relevant stakeholders to ensure a prompt and effective response. In all these cases, failing to identify key details quickly resulted in insufficient response measures and negative consequences, such as loss of life, environmental damage, and long-term economic impact.

"ME" Resetting and Reframing in a Crisis

It is natural to feel overwhelmed and out of control when confronted with a crisis; however, as a leader, it is critical to maintain a calm and confident demeanour to keep those around you from panicking. By initiating self-control exercises, such as counting to ten and taking deep breaths, you can trigger your own "code-blue" alert and begin to recognize and understand the initial level of the crisis you are facing.

Remember that your behaviour sets the tone for those around you. If you panic, others will follow suit; if you remain calm and composed, others will do the same. As a result, it is critical to develop the "mental" muscle to be fully efficient in a crisis. You can do this by taking personal time to assess your reactions to emergency scenarios, creating scripts and mentally rehearsing different situations, and figuring out how to reset quickly.

To accomplish this, quickly imagine simple scenarios that might trigger emotional reactions, such as an office confrontation or a life-threatening emergency, to embed in your memory bank. With regular practice, you will be able to withdraw from these mental exercises quickly and efficiently, just like athletes who use continuous mental exercises to discipline their bodies. Navigating through life, I have come to understand the profound impact of emotions on our perception. There have been instances when my own feelings have cast a veil over my vision, obscuring the intricate forces at play in shaping the course of events.

Because of this, I have learned the importance of cultivating healthy emotional coping mechanisms. These mechanisms become the anchors that keep you steady, preventing emotions from becoming blinding barriers. I have found that this practice is akin to clearing a path through a dense forest. By honing these coping mechanisms, I have been able to hack away at the emotional underbrush and gain a clearer view of the landscape. This clarity has enabled me to navigate challenges with greater insight and effectiveness.

Through the years, I have come to treasure these coping mechanisms as invaluable companions, guiding me through the tumultuous seas of crisis and offering me the clarity I need to discern the broader picture.

By reframing the situation and focusing on the other forces at work, you can reset and mobilize creativity, reflection, and analytics as you move between the various levels of urgencies confronting you and your team. Two of the most significant sources of such influences during a crisis are our relationships and the social environment. Our mental filters can sometimes lead us to see only what we want to see, ignoring facts and realities that do not fit our preconceived notions. Denial can also be a dangerous response, allowing us to avoid confronting unpleasant realities and making faulty decisions.

Natural and human-caused disasters create a dynamic and unpredictable environment, and effective crisis leadership necessitates constantly evaluating organizational structures and response capacities. While routine emergencies may have a hierarchical command-and-control structure and established standard operating procedures, extreme events can push an organization beyond its operational limits, resulting in unexpected events, such as the 9/11 attacks, that overwhelm even the best emergency response systems, making understanding an organization's operational limits critical for effective crisis leadership.

Leaders who lack such knowledge cannot effectively manage their organization's response to the crisis. Leadership during times of crisis is distinctly different from leadership in normal circumstances due to several factors. These include the heightened importance and potential consequences of decisions, increased scrutiny from the public, unpredictable emotions and attitudes, and fewer rigid institutional restrictions on the decision-making authority of those in positions of power.

"ME" and My Emotional Intelligence: IQ vs. EQ

Stress is unavoidable during times of crisis; however, it is critical to manage our reactions to reduce their impact on our lives and those we manage. Your emotional responses can have a broad impact, and staying in control and being a model of sustained calm under pressure is essential.

While many people connect intelligence with a high intelligence quotient (IQ), great leaders require both IQ and emotional intelligence (EQ); they must operate together. It enables cognitive development. For me, emotional intelligence is more than just a concept; it is a skill that I have embraced as a vital part of my personal growth. It is about understanding, harnessing, and steering my emotions in ways that contribute positively to my life's journey. EQ acts as a sort of compass, guiding me through the intricate labyrinth of experiences. It is like having a map that helps me navigate the terrain of stress, enabling effective communication, and fostering genuine empathy towards others.

In my quest to develop emotional intelligence, I have encountered its power to transform challenges into opportunities. It is as if this skill gives me the tools to defuse conflicts, overcome obstacles, and find my way through setbacks and failures.

However, it was the realization of its practical significance that truly sparked a change within me. It was not just about understanding emotions; it was about utilizing them as a force for good, both for myself and in my interactions with others.

This journey of cultivating emotional intelligence has been deeply personal. It is like a canvas on which I have painted my own growth, layer by layer, embracing the difficulties, the triumphs, and challenges. Each step has led me closer to a state of balance and resilience, where emotions serve as allies rather than obstacles.

Peter Salovey and John D. Mayer first introduced the concept of emotional intelligence in their 1990 article titled "Emotional Intelligence" in the journal *Imagination, Cognition, and Personality.*"[21] American psychologist Daniel Goleman popularized this idea in his 1995 book *Emotional Intelligence: Why It Can Matter More than IQ.*

Mastering our emotional responses proves essential when confronting intense circumstances, like delivering or receiving feedback, working within tight time limits, managing intricate relationships, addressing limited resources, or navigating the ever-shifting tides of change. Daniel Goleman emphasizes the importance of four key branches of emotional intelligence in times of crisis: self-awareness, self-management, social awareness, and relationship management.[22]

Emotional intelligence refers to the ability to understand, utilize, and effectively manage emotions in a positive manner, allowing individuals to experience stress relief, engage in effective communication, demonstrate empathy toward others, overcome challenges, resolve conflicts, and navigate setbacks and failures.

Self-management necessitates brain training to strengthen the prefrontal cortex's ability to exert control over the amygdala, the fight-or-flight section of the brain that responds quickly to threats. Mindfulness exercises have been shown in studies to improve leaders' resilience, resulting in emotionally balanced and effective leadership.

Leaders must deal with people from varied backgrounds, cultures, and professions, and creating long-term connections across the field is part of the engagement skills required to manage such crises. Relationship management requires the ability to inspire others, manage conflicts, foster teamwork, and move people in the desired direction; each of these competencies necessitates self-awareness, self-control, and social awareness.

---

21 Peter Salovey and James D. Mayer, "Emotional Intelligence," Imagination, Cognition and Personality 9, no. 3 (1990): 185–211, https://doi.org/10.2190/DUGG-P24E-52WK-6CDG.

22 Daniel Goleman, "4 Emotional Intelligence Skills for Trying Times," Korn Ferry Institute, accessed November 10, 2023, https://www.kornferry.com/insights/briefings-for-the-boardroom/4-emotional-intelligence-skills-for-trying-times.

During a crisis, it is critical to prioritize self-care. Just as flight attendants instruct passengers to put on their own masks before helping others, leaders must first take care of themselves before helping others. Neglecting one's well-being and rushing to help others may not be the best approach. Instead, leaders should prioritize their own oxygen mask before moving on to helping others. It takes time and work to develop emotional intelligence competencies, but the benefits are well worth it; increasing our emotional intelligence can help us get through the next crisis much more smoothly.

"ME" Using the Best of the Seven Habits in Times of Crisis

Personal Log: Fort McMurray, Alberta, May 3, 2016, 8:30 p.m. to 11:00 p.m.: Through Hell!

With our property secured, my wife, our anxious puppy Jaxx, and I hit the highway towards Anzac, a community located 50 km south of Fort McMurray, hoping to regroup. The traffic, however, crawled at a snail's pace, and I could not help but worry as embers flew around us from nearby trees and grass fires. Despite the danger, we remained orderly and focused on the road ahead, which was inundated with cars, SUVs, and trucks.

My fuel gauge showed less than a quarter of gas. There are no cities, villages, or gas stations between Fort McMurray and Wandering River (325 km apart).

As we approached the south side of town, my relief was palpable as our properties, the Radisson, and Vantage Hotels, still stood tall. Sadly, our competitor's property, the Super 8, continued to burn.

During our slow crawl on the highway, I monitored our evacuation team's progress via my cell phone. Our team was moving to temporary shelters in various locations, and Mike and Colleen were doing an excellent job of tracking their movements. Ryan Melnyk, our regional sales manager, was securing space with our sister properties throughout Alberta and sourcing additional space at competitive properties and universities through his valuable contacts. At that point, they had confirmed the location and status of almost 90 percent of our team members. My top priority was to ensure every-one's safety. I used all my resources, via my team leaders, to synchro-nize and coordinate proper relocation.

This was at the forefront of my mind to make sure everyone knew we had their best interests in these very trying times. I wanted to make sure they felt supported, as I knew later that I would need their full support once again to come back stronger than ever. I reviewed constantly in my mind what my options were in the present and started to work on different scenarios that would help us all. We inched closer to Anzac; a drive that typically takes forty minutes took us two and a half hours because of the dire circumstances. I felt grateful to emerge from the situation alive with my wife and puppy in tow. A safe temporary refuge was coming together for all our team members, their families, and pets.

The classic *the 7 Habits of Highly Effective People* by Stephen R. Covey is one book that I frequently return to. The book highlights seven habits: (1) being pro-active, (2) beginning with the end in mind, (3) putting things first, (4) thinking win-win, (5) seeking first to understand and then to be understood, (6) synergizing, and (7) sharpening the saw.[23]

To foster a team-first environment, it is critical to establish trust between leaders and teams. Lack of trust during a crisis can lead to gossip, resentment, and a lack of accountability. "A genuine leader is not a searcher for consensus but a molder for consensus.[24] The leader should shape every-one's opinion into a consensus that is embraced by all. Everyone should come together and prevent rumours from circulating. Respect is earned daily and requires practice. We can achieve this by being patient and learn-ing to listen to all levels within the organization.

Long ago, I decided not to be a clown for any company. This means that I do not focus on making everyone happy and jolly but on being respected

---

23   Steven R. Covey, The 7 Habits of Highly Effective People (Simon & Shuster) New York, 2020), 52.

24   Henna Inam, "Martin Luther King on Leadership: 10 Quotes for a Changing World," Forbes, April 4,2018, https://forbes.com/sites/hennainam/2018/04/04/ martin-luther-king-on-leadership-ten-quotes-for-a-changing-world/?sh=69415bc75c88.

through my authenticity and asking for accountability while being consistent in my judgments and decisions.

Building a network of resources is also important in times of crisis. As discussed later in this book, building local relationships with municipal businesses, political personnel, and governmental entities takes time but adds value in times of need. As a leader, it is critical to be of service to all.

With authenticity and prominent levels of trust, the team will be comfortable making tough decisions; the team will take these decisions at face value, quickly assess them, and then move on. When a crisis occurs in a "service to all" mentally oriented organization, instinct takes over initial panic, and a solutions' mindset comes into action, rather than rash decisions.

Personal Reflections on "ME"

It's been a few years since the events took place, and I sometimes ask myself if, as a leader, I did the best I could and where I could have done better for all concerned. Initially, in the first hours of these crises, I was shocked and frustrated, and could not believe how quickly the event unfolded around me, affecting so many of us in a matter of a few hours.

The impact was hard to grasp at the beginning, but I knew it would have terrible consequences for us and our families. I had to think quickly and decisively while looking out for the interests of all team members and their families. There was a sense of urgency I imposed on myself to address and protect the interests of the owners and organization as well. As the enormity of the crisis unfolded, I had some initial anxieties about how this would affect our jobs, lives, and futures.

In the first hours of the crisis, I focused on gathering as much relevant and valid information as possible on what factors were not in my control and which options I would have under my control. Initially, I did not feel overwhelmed, but I did feel powerless and frustrated by not taking more initiative. I quickly realized that most of what was happening was out of my control.

I had to assess the extent of the crisis from as much information as I could gather, but I kept an open mind, filtered the flow of information I received, and kept the most valuable information to benefit my team and organization. Understanding quickly that this crisis would be a mid- to long-term situation where we would be uprooted to a different living and working environment, I had to address the basic needs of everyone after lodging, which are the financial concerns of the team and ownership. I was anxious to get everyone out unharmed. This had to be addressed and communicated to all concerned. Going through so many emotions, I had to maintain a sense of calm and composure. I wanted to make sure that everyone, including the team and ownership, knew I had the situation under relative control to instill confidence and stability as we were all going through uncharted waters.

As all of us were working in separate locations, towns, and regions, I wanted to make sure I had the proper channel of communication to provide immediate support and reassurance while being brutally honest about our situation. I had to make sure that proper and reliable information was communicated in a firm, timely, and disciplined manner through the entire evacuation and re-entry later.

PART TWO:
"US" THROUGH HELL AND HIGH WATER

"US" Leading and Influencing Others

Personal Log: Anzac, Alberta, May 4, 2016. Through Hell!

We joined a flow of evacuees in the small community of Anzac south of Fort McMurray. We met some of my team members who decided to stay there rather than drive further south or north. We compared notes on who was where and progresses on their relocation. We were all doing the best we could surrounded by unknowns and angst. Our first night was spent in our car, but my cell phone was constantly ringing with updates and confirmation of team members and families relocation status.

Shortly after midnight, a firefighter who had been urgently dispatched from Calgary to help his much-battered brothers-in-arms in Fort McMurray called me. He was told he could use our properties to get some sleep. Having tried to go to one of our properties that had lost power, I then directed him via phone to my prime property, the Clearwater Suite Hotel, two blocks from where he was. I gave him a quick lesson in programming electronic hotel room doors and felt good about being able to help those coming to save our livelihood. I can speak on behalf of all the hoteliers in the world that no matter what circumstances we go through, a hotelier is primarily a host. It is in our DNA.

Not getting a second of sleep, I contacted the assistant fire chief, whom I knew from local safety board committees. He confirmed that all our properties were standing, but there would be damage from smoke and water, as water bomber planes were attempting to win the battle against the "Beast." I communicated this news to the ownership and management company, and settled in the community centre, as we thought we would be there for the night and go home the next day.

The "Beast" had other ideas. With the help of intense winds, it won territory over dried forest and grass, advancing towards the airport and the township of Anzac, where we had initially evacuated. By 4:00 p.m., the skies were pitch-black from smoke and the news was not encouraging.

I then connected with all the general managers via conference call for a status report. All were in good spirits, even those who had lost their homes and were settling in various locations. I informed them of the situation as I knew it and confirmed that all our properties were still standing, but some might have sustained severe water damage because of the water bomber's actions. I asked them to communicate with their team members and families about the ownership and management concerns regarding their safety and well-being after these terrible events. We were then informed that the fire was gaining ground at the airport and that some auxiliary buildings, hangars, and a recently built hotel across the runway had already been destroyed. Some properties in Anzac were now on fire.

We were once again under a mandatory evacuation order!

The grass and trees surrounding the community centre started to burn. The city had wisely moved buses from their downtown location to our community centre. Having a limited amount of gas in my car, we opted to travel by city bus to our next destination, Edmonton. Leaving Anzac, we saw gigantic reddish flares on the horizon, shadowed by ominous smoke and dark skies. I then realized we may not see our home or properties for a while, and this was not a temporary escape anymore but a full-fledged evacuation.

During times of crisis, a leader must travel via multiple organizational levels within their team. Coordination and the leverage of influence are critical in such situations. Creating settings that encourage shared values, motivate constituents, and inspire them to contribute to the overall objective and vision will provide enormous rewards. People buy into the leader before the vision in any organization. As a result, cultivating a team-first environment is critical. Building a team is crucial and will be discussed further in this book, but it becomes even more important during times of crisis due to the intricacies and urgency of the situation.

Traditional organizations are gradually being replaced by more open, independent strategic units. Diverse cultures offer their own set of expectations and techniques and harmonizing them can be difficult; however, effective leadership may align these units in a productive order.

"US" and Influence over Authority

Why would you choose to lead others?
Making a difference or finding purpose provides meaning in society. Some people may be motivated by self-centred reasons, such as attaining wealth, power, or notoriety. True leadership, on the other hand, inspires, motivates, and engages others. Genuine leaders add value and enthusiasm to the people around them. They provide solutions and care about the people in their sphere of influence, resulting in a reciprocal relationship.

In his most famous book, *the 21 Irrefutable Laws of Leadership*, John C. Maxwell says that "Leadership is influence. No more, no less!"[25]

Influence is a critical element to manage, especially during times of crisis when one must navigate uncharted seas between authority and influence. The right to impose activities on others, decide, and issue commands is associated with authority, whereas influence is associated with emotional intelligence. Others bestow authority on you; however, influence comes from within. You will gain greater authority as you advance in your job and move up the executive ladder. This can be evident in your capacity to hire your own team; design and implement company plans, policies, and laws; and even let go of individuals who no longer match the common

---

25   John S. Luna, review of , The 21 Irrefutable Laws of Leadership: Follow Them and People Will Follow You, by John C. Maxwell, Occupational Therapy in Health Care 36, no. 4 (September 30, 2021): 494–96, https://doi.org/10.1080/07380577.2021.1983240.

goals and vision. You gain unambiguous power over your subordinates and work toward agreed-upon missions and goals.

However, leadership is more than just having power. It demands a perfect balance of both authority and influence. Your authority is obtained from outside resources. Your reputation, as well as the company will reflect and depend on the internal efforts and resources of others. This is when influence comes into play.

$$\text{Capacity to produce results} = \text{Authority} + \text{Influence}$$

You got outcomes and results because you wanted them, not because they were needed. Listening to others, demonstrating flexibility and openness, and encouraging persuasion and inspiration are all crucial characteristics of a powerful leader.

We cannot delegate or appoint authority or influence. Influence must be gained. Leadership is concerned with persuading others to follow you, whereas management is concerned with sustaining systems and processes.

True leadership starts from the inside. It describes the leader's personality. Concentrate on your actions and attitudes. Remember that you are being watched, listened to, and judged during times of crisis. Be honest with yourself and receptive to other people's perspectives. True leadership is also about relationships. The saying "He who thinks he leads but has no followers is only taking a walk" emphasizes the necessity of influencing followers.

Share credit and be consistent with the people you work with. Finally, great leadership is about knowledge. "Knowledge is power", as Sir Francis Bacon once remarked, and you must have a thorough awareness of the facts and dynamics involved in a crisis to respond correctly. True leadership is about acquiring respect through authenticity and genuineness. As a leader, you must value being respected over being loved.

"US" and Managing Order and Chaos

Overseeing a crisis demands a keen understanding of priorities, the capacity to manage multiple components, and the ability to manoeuvre through uncertainty.

You must decide what is significant and what is not, assess what others are doing, and plan for future implications. To do so, you must behave like a detective on the scene, reacting to changes and techniques. This is not the time to be dogmatic or linear in your thinking. Instead, it is critical to ask questions, empathize with the individuals affected, give solutions, and gather clues and new possibilities to make informed decisions. A crisis is a fluid scenario that requires involvement from all parties concerned to add more perspectives to the conversation.

Personal Log: Fort McMurray, Alberta, May 3 to May 5, 2016: Through Hell!

Chad Beaton, senior manager of Canadian Natural's Horizon Oil Sands mine on the northside of Fort McMurray, played a critical role in coordinating the evacuation. He recalls receiving thirty-five hundred individuals and their pets and flying out twenty-seven hundred people in a sixteen-hour period to Calgary and Edmonton on May 3 and May 4. The evacuees arrived with everything, including newborns, families, friends, and animals, and the crew did everything they could to care for everyone. Beaton also had the vital role of keeping his team on site to preserve calm and order, even though some of them had arrived from other parts of the country and had no idea where they were in relation to the fire.

Suncor Energy director of transportation, travel, and strategy, Fauzia Lalani, says that they initially thought they would only be able to aid a few people, but the problem proved to be far greater than they had anticipated. Suncor was the first major gathering site for those who could not migrate south, and they had access to many camp facilities, including their own lodges, which quickly filled up. They had over ten thousand rooms, many of which hosted numerous residents, including pets of all types, from dogs and cats to pot-bellied pigs, ferrets, fish, rabbits, and more. To address the requirements of the evacuees, they immediately turned lobbies, kitchens, and cafeterias into makeshift sleeping and eating places.

Upon reflection, I realized the magnitude of the joint effort required from all stakeholders engaged to properly respond to the Fort McMurray wildfire catastrophe. The circumstances required flexibility, empathy, quick decision-making abilities, and I was impressed to see how well the responders met the task.

As flames raged dangerously near the oil sands plants, it was critical to cooperate with WestJet to facilitate the evacuation of evacueess from the landing strips to Edmonton. The safety of all those affected was paramount, and the responders' efforts were admirable.

This event has highlighted the importance of being well prepared for any disaster and ensuring that emergency preparations include not only humans but all components, such as pets.

"US" Confronting Order and Disorder

It is critical to be aware of ongoing dynamics, but it is also critical to develop a foundation of credibility through internal processes and hierarchies. Order offers a sense of security and predictability by establishing expectations and obligations.

Ordering roles, norms, and responsibilities can produce positive results, but too much order can stifle innovation, adaptation, and involvement. Leaders must retain an agile mind and be willing to pivot from established scenarios.

Disorder and order can coexist. Some people have a messy desk but can find a specific document among a sea of papers and files. Creating order through expectations is crucial, but in times of crisis, leaders should not be paralyzed by disarray. During a crisis, chaos and anarchy can be beneficial. While control and command may appear to be the reaction to disorder, the desire to overcontrol people can reduce one's chances of success. To avoid failure, open communication is critical during times of crisis. Some people thrive in turmoil, while others struggle.

Political leaders have utilized turmoil to disrupt societal order to impose their own political rule; however, influence can swiftly restore order. It is critical to engage your team and avoid taking a commanding position.

Being involved and included in the process might promote flexibility in the path the leader desires to take. It is critical to balance determination with sensitivity, perseverance while listening, and comprehending others team members perspectives.

As previously stated, amid a crisis, perfection is unattainable, and leaders must demonstrate vulnerability and humility. Being vulnerable and humble will help build trust, but authenticity is essential. People follow those they trust, not because of their authority or prestige. When trust is built, there is an exchange of values between parties, and everyone benefits from each other's devotion to a common purpose. Trust is the cornerstone of influence, which is the foundation of establishing order.

"US" and the Trust Factor

In my previous logs, I attempted to emphasize the value of working and thinking as a team. As our Fort McMurray hotel portfolio expanded from three to eight buildings, I realized the need to establish a culture of unity that capitalized on our strength of owning 40 percent of the town's hotel room inventory. I attempted to instill a positive team spirit in a group of people from various origins, levels of professionalism, ethnicities, and social upbringings.

To achieve this goal, I searched through my collection of previously read books in various boxes and from my bookcases, and unearthed Patrick M. Lencioni's, *"The Five Dysfunctions of a Team,"* which I highly suggest to any team leader. As per Lencioni's insights, effective teamwork hinges on mastering five fundamental pillars. The book delves into these pillars, illustrating how teams can falter when these elements are not cultivated, presenting a dynamic model of dysfunction in five interconnected parts. Teams or organizations that lack trust, are afraid of healthy disagreements, lack commitment, evade accountability, and pay no attention to results, will become dysfunctional and produce poor results.[26]

I collaborated with a local vocational college to establish a program tailored to our needs. We highlighted and continued to implement these core ideas every day throughout our entire organization with the help of one of my local business acquaintances who was in semi-retirement and served as a coach on this subject. The deep level of trust we all shared among ourselves and with other disciplines had a significant impact on

---

26 Patrick Lencioni, "Teamwork: The Five Dysfunctions of a Team," The Table Group, accessed November 11, 2023, https://www.tablegroup.com/topics-and-resources/teamwork-5-dysfunctions.

our capacity to work as a unique cluster of properties and leaders. We were charged with selecting a name for ourselves during the early courses of the program, and the term "Team WOne" (a Winning Team of One) symbolized who we were to be. This group cohesiveness and elevated level of trust among ourselves has been essential in our collective evacuation in May 2016, our handling of the floods in 2020, and our capacity to traverse the pandemic and economic slump.

During unusual times, trust is critical. It provides a sense of predictability in both known and unfamiliar situations. Author Patrick Lencioni is also the founder and president of The Table Group, a consulting firm focused on establishing healthy companies. He emphasizes the importance of trust being linked to a sense of vulnerability and transparency formed and acknowledged by all members of an effective team. When genuine members can raise their hands and ask for help or admit, "I screwed up," or "This is a good idea," without fear of punishment or grudges, you have a truly united team ready to face any obstacles thrown their way.

You cannot go through a crisis by yourself; you need a trusted team. Having a trusted network around you in times of instability will be critical to your individual and group success.

Establishing trust will provide you with a stable foundation from which to examine what is going on around you. Trust will clarify complexities while providing mutual assistance. It fosters mutual respect and confidence, as well as accuracy and dependability.

However, the word "team" has many distinct meanings, situations, and interpretations. There is a significant difference between a team and a working group. Most teams are just that: a working group! Think of a golf foursome where each golfer plays their own game, and they add the total up of individual scores. A real team is more like a basketball team, where each team member plays together simultaneously, exchanging roles, positions, and responsibilities on the court while playing their own style.

During times of crisis, it is critical to have a *small* and effective leadership team known as the emergency response team (ERT) that work collaboratively to achieve common organizational objectives. The emphasis on small is vital since too many team members can cause logistical concerns and communication breakdowns. Confronted with suggested number of members to sit on a board or committee, I frequently used the image of a camel which could have been a horse designed by a dysfunctional and large committee. Smaller teams bring clarity and a sense of urgency. To eliminate confusion or disinformation, the ERT must work together and have a keen sense of alignment and trust among themselves.

To avoid dissatisfaction and despair, timely and unambiguous communication must be cascaded across the organization. Polling team members at various levels to check that the message has been comprehended and executed can help maintain clarity and unity. The messaging must then be cascaded within specific groups. Any business must embed goals, roles and duties. Throughout his work as an organizational development and transformation consultant, Noel Tichy explored how team conflicts emerge using a framework centered around goals, roles, processes, and interactions. He emphasized the cascading nature of these conflicts, highlighting their far-reaching implications.

According to the paper The GRPI Model—An Approach for Team Development,

> [Tichy] observed a ratio of 80:20 per cent of conflicts accumulating at each level: he observed that 80% of team conflicts come from unclear goals. Of the remaining 20%, four out of five conflicts come from unclear roles. Unclear processes caused 80% of the remaining conflicts. Finally, only 1% of the conflicts in teams can be attributed to interpersonal relationships.[27]

As a result, having clear objectives and well-defined roles and duties can help avoid conflicts and boost productivity.

Because trust is such a vital topic, I want to suggest some techniques and strategies to assist you in developing a dependable foundation for interacting with your team. Building trust within your business is akin to taking a daily shower or bath. It demands on your part consistencies in your written or verbal deliveries and repetitive actions.

---

27   Steve Raue, Suk-Han Tang, Christian Weiland, and Claas Wenzik, The GRPI Model—An Approach for Team Development (Berlin-Mitte: Systemic Excellence Group, 2013), 6.

Accountability is a necessary attribute for individuals and organizations to succeed, especially during times of crisis. Those with high degrees of accountability take ownership of problems within their control and seek new methods to overcome them. Those who are below the line, on the other hand, focus on what is out of their control, blame others, and make excuses, inhibiting innovation, and forward thinking.

Leaders must complete a four-step approach to exceed the required standards:

Recognize the situation. Accept reality and bring everyone together to find answers.

Embrace psychological ownership of the problem, allowing individuals to focus on what they have control over. You "own" the issues, concerns, and consequences of your actions or worst your own inactions.

Devise novel solutions to the problems. You need to think creatively to find immediate system, processes, and tools for your team to succeed in the immediacy of the crisis.

Act in the face of uncertainty. You must get the buy-in of your peers by encouraging them to execute your vision and tasks. Rising above the line necessitates purposeful optimism, in which individuals understand the existing reality but extend optimistic faith that all will work out if they focus on the things they can influence positively.

Accountability is required not only from executives but also from employees throughout the firm, as it stimulates creativity and positive thinking and leads to a more creative work environment. Creating a sense of connection and belonging is critical in developing a productive work environment, especially during times of crisis.

Recognize and validate your employees' feelings and reactions. By acknowledging and validating their emotions and behaviours, the leader demonstrates knowledge of the issues they confront and a willingness in working together to overcome them. In my experience as a leader, I have learned the incredible value of involving my team in decision-making processes. It is like opening a door to a realm of shared empowerment and collaboration. When I extended an invitation for input, I witnessed a remarkable transformation within my team. It is as if this act kindles a spark of ownership and progress. The sense of empowerment that arises, fosters an environment where everyone feels invested, contributing not just as individuals but as an integrated force. Team WOne executive meetings were always lively: we had healthy debates where everyone's contribution was valued.

I have found that this approach has a profound impact on motivation and engagement. When team members have a say in choices that shape our path, they are more than just participants; they become cocreators of your collective journey. Their dedication and enthusiasm soars, breathing life into our shared endeavours.

Involving my staff in decision-making has become a cornerstone of my leadership philosophy. It is a testament to the power of unity, the strength that surfaces when each voice contributes to the benefit of all.

Ensure that team members do not become lost in the crowd. One method is to limit team sizes and, to the greatest extent possible, acknowledge each member's labour and successes. This strengthens the bond and stimulates dialogue.

Leaders should provide opportunities for employees to demonstrate their understanding of a particular activity or skill. This helps to boost confidence and reinforce expertise.

When difficulties develop, seek complete feedback from those concerned. This aids in identifying the most pressing concerns and difficulties, as well as strengthening the bond between team members.

Regular check-ins have also become a cornerstone of my approach. It is more than just discussing progress on individual goals; it is about crafting a space where aspirations are heard, acknowledged, and nurtured. These conversations are like watering the seeds of growth, where we collaboratively devise strategies to help each team member flourish.

By prioritizing these interactions, I have witnessed a profound shift in the workplace dynamic. It is as if a bridge forms between the personal and professional realms, allowing us to recognize each other's humanity amidst the pursuit of goals. This bridge becomes a conduit for trust, respect, and shared commitment.

My leadership style is anchored in the belief that when we prioritize our team members' well-being, we pave the way for not only enhanced productivity but also a work environment that is fueled by empathy and mutual support. This helps to keep staff motivated and engaged while also providing opportunities for feedback and progress. In times of crisis, connection is critical for maintaining a healthy work environment. By adopting these measures, leaders may help employees feel cared for and valued, which can develop a sense of belonging and promote effective teamwork.

Competence is another crucial part of employee motivation and satisfaction. Employees who feel effective and grow are more likely to be engaged and productive. Promoting competency is crucial for retaining employee engagement and satisfaction, especially during times of crisis. This can lead to higher productivity and engagement. Leaders should empower their employees to feel in charge of their actions and decisions, which should be aligned with their own values, ambitions, and interests, as well as those of their team. I have come to recognize the profound impact of encouraging individuality and fostering a genuine concern for my team. It is like creating a nurturing space where everyone's unique strengths and contributions are valued, while still holding onto the collective responsibility of achieving team goals.

Micromanaging, I have found, is a surefire way to stifle creativity and dishearten employees, especially during trying times. As a leader, I have learned to tread lightly, allowing space for autonomy to flourish. This belief in autonomy has led me to embrace several guiding principles.

In my daily interactions with my teams, I have learned the power of language. Instead of using dominating phrases that induce pressure, I have shifted toward motivation through positive reinforcement. Encouraging words like "I have total faith in you and your team" have a magical way of instilling confidence and fostering a supportive atmosphere.

Transparency has been another key pillar. By explaining the rationale behind tasks, I have witnessed a boost in engagement. When people understand the "why" behind their efforts, they are more likely to invest their energy wholeheartedly.

This emphasis on autonomy is not just a strategy; it is a recognition of the interconnected web between relatedness, competence, and autonomy. These channels are like conduits that can either flow freely or become clogged in our work environment. In moments of difficulty, I have noticed that motivation can be quite delicate. That's why I make it a priority to foster these pathways, ensuring my team experiences a sense of connection and belonging, discovers purpose and development (self-learnings), and possess confidence and empowerment in their abilities to self-determination.

My journey as a leader is anchored in creating an environment where each team member's individuality is celebrated, their growth is nurtured, and their autonomy is respected. Through this approach, I have witnessed not just enhanced engagement, but a shared commitment to excellence that propelled us forward, even in the face of adversity.

"US" Managing Optimism, Vision, and Confidence in Times of Crisis

The Stockdale Protocol, also known as the Stockdale Paradox, is a concept named after Admiral James Stockdale, who was a United States Navy vice admiral and aviator. The protocol is often associated with crisis management, particularly in the context of personal resilience and leadership during challenging situations.[28]

The Stockdale Protocol was derived from Admiral Stockdale's experiences as a prisoner of war in Vietnam, during the Vietnam War. He was held captive in the infamous Hanoi Hilton prison for over seven years, enduring extreme physical and psychological torture. Despite the harsh conditions, Stockdale survived and helped other fellow prisoners to survive under horrible circumstances as well.

The Stockdale Protocol consists of two key principles:

1. *Confront the brutal facts.* Stockdale believed that facing the harsh realities of a crisis or challenging situation head-on is essential. Denying or avoiding the truth of the situation can lead to unrealistic expectations and misguided decisions. Acknowledging the difficulties, no matter how painful, allows individuals and leaders to make informed decisions and take effective action.

---

28   Boris Groysberg and Robin Abrahams, "What the Stockdale Paradox Tell Us about Crisis Leadership." Harvard Business School, August 17, 2020.

2. *Maintain faith and hope.* Alongside confronting the brutal facts, Stockdale emphasized the importance of maintaining faith and hope in the ultimate outcome. He noticed that those who were overly optimistic and expected immediate rescue were often the ones who struggled the most when their expectations were not met.

Balancing a realistic assessment of the situation with a steadfast belief that one can overcome the challenges is crucial for enduring and succeeding in a crisis.

While the Stockdale Protocol emphasizes endurance and persistence, it encourages individuals and organizations to keep their sights on long-term goals even in the face of immediate challenges. This perspective can prevent knee-jerk reactions and guide actions that lead to sustainable solutions.

Adopting the paradox promotes an adaptable culture. Organizations that promote a culture of receptiveness to novelty and change are more adept at manoeuvring through periods of unpredictability. One can develop greater adaptability by actively seeking out novel approaches and solutions. Crises provide invaluable learning and development opportunities. Organizations and individuals who embrace the Stockdale Paradox methodology are more inclined to engage in introspection, discern valuable insights, and employ them as a bedrock for subsequent progress. Both organizations and individuals are encouraged to maintain a long-term perspective by the paradox. It is essential, while addressing immediate obstacles, to maintain perspective on the large picture and strive for long-term success.

According to research by psychologist John Leach and others, people who escape disasters "regain cognitive function swiftly, assess their unfamiliar surroundings accurately, and engage in goal-directed action to survive within it."[29] This is true for both wildfires and plane crashes.

The Stockdale Paradox underscores a delicate equilibrium: acknowledging the realities that demand relinquishing presumed control while retaining an inherent drive to endure.

---

29   Laurence Gonzales, "Deep Survival, Who Lives, Who Dies and Why," WGYT with Sean Delaney, accessed on January 24, 2024, https://whatgotyouthere.com/deep-survival-who-lives-who-dies-and-why-by-laurence-gonzales-book-recap/.

"US" and Our Sense of Vision

In times of crisis, having an unclouded vision is critical because it provides a clear line of sight, encourages optimism, and allows for effective decision-making.

Your team will require immediate directions and guidance in the event of a crisis. Your vision will provide them with a road map: steps to take as they will feel powerless. Your vision will also provide a much-appreciated sense of hope above reigning chaos and confusion, as well as confirming common goals.

Motivation and inspiration. Your vision will serve as a source of motivation, encouragement, for them, their family, and friends, confirming a feeling of purpose and hope, providing them something to strive for in the face of hardship.

Decision-making and prioritization. Be decisive while addressing what are the most urgent steps needed to be taken according to your vision; changing your mind will create even more confusion. Be assertive while being receptive to concerns.

Adaptability and resilience. The ability to navigate rapidly changing circumstances is frequently required during crises. A strong vision acts as a North Star, allowing individuals and organizations to adjust their strategies and tactics while remaining true to their core values and aspirations. It fosters resilience by providing a sense of stability and direction in the face of uncertainty.

Unity and collaboration. During a crisis, a compelling vision can unite people and foster collaboration. When individuals share a common vision, they are more likely to work together, share resources, and support one another towards achieving a collective goal, which increases the effectiveness of crisis response efforts and promotes a sense of unity within communities.

Align vision and purpose. This is critical for providing individuals and organizations with a sense of direction and meaning. Many events beyond your control will pull you away from your vision and purpose, and it is critical that you revisit frequently your core values.

I suggest the following steps:

Revisit and clarify purpose. Begin by revisiting the purpose of your organization or the purpose that drives you as an individual. Consider the core values, principles, and why you do what you do. During a crisis, it is wise to reaffirm and clearly articulate your purpose to ensure it remains relevant and meaningful in the face of adversity.

Assess the current situation. Evaluate the impact of the crisis on your organization or personal circumstances. Understand the challenges, risks, and opportunities that arise from this event. Assess how your purpose aligns with the current reality and identify any gaps or adjustments required to respond effectively.

Define or refine the vision. Based on your purpose and understanding of the crisis context, define or refine your vision. A vision should be aspirational, forward-looking, and aligned with your purpose. It should inspire and motivate, providing a clear image of the desired future state. Ensure that the vision reflects the values, aspirations, and positive impact you hope to achieve despite the crisis.

Communicate and engage. Effectively communicate the vision and purpose to all stakeholders. Open and transparent communication is critical to building trust, alignment, and engagement. Clearly articulate how the vision and purpose connect with the current crisis and emphasize how they provide a sense of direction and hope.

Align strategies and actions. Review your strategies and actions considering the vision and purpose to ensure that they are aligned and contribute to the overall direction. Identify areas that require adjustment or reprioritization to address immediate crisis needs while still upholding the long-term vision. Continuously evaluate and adapt your strategies to align with the evolving crisis landscape.

Empower and involve others. Engage and empower individuals within your organization or community to contribute to the vision and purpose alignment. Encourage their input, ideas, and initiatives that align with the overarching vision. Foster a sense of ownership and collective responsibility, as it is critical to have a united front during challenging times.

Monitor progress and learn. Regularly monitor progress toward vision and purpose alignment. Assess the impact of actions taken and make necessary adjustments. Learn from both successes and failures to continuously improve and adapt. Encourage a culture of learning, resilience, and innovation within the organization or community.

By aligning vision with purpose during times of crisis, you lay a firm foundation for resilience, direction, and meaning, assisting individuals and organizations in navigating through problems, inspiring collective action, and working toward a better future.

Our vision during the wildfires was "Team WOne: Strong, Supportive, United, and Resilient." It carried us and continued to do so long after we returned to Fort McMurray.

"US" and Our Confidence

While it is encouraging to see hope during a crisis, it is critical to persevere and constantly assess your leadership team and employees, demonstrating your confidence in their actions. You will regain your self-confidence as you and your team develop, but doubts will seep in along the way.

While you do not want to instill fear in your team, being overly positive can come across as dismissive of the challenges they are facing. It is critical to acknowledge the difficulties everyone is experiencing and avoid attempting to bypass or ignore them. Individuals and teams can overcome even the most difficult circumstances by being realistic about the situation while maintaining a sense of faith and determination.

During a crisis like the COVID-19 pandemic, people may have experienced it in diverse ways, depending on a variety of factors, such as their location, family situation, and expectations; it is critical to keep these key factors in mind while leading your team.

From my experience, I have come to understand that every crisis presents its unique challenges; however, what remains strikingly consistent are the core leadership qualities that guide a team through effective crisis management. It is like a timeless compass that points the way, regardless of the storm we find ourselves navigating.

COVID-19, or similar events, differ from a fire or a flood, but the skills to deal with chaos are the same. Leaders must be decisive and take control of the situation, exercise caution, and stay positive at the same time. When sifting through the initial data and bits of information gathered at the start of a crisis, the best thing we can do is communicate to our team that we value their safety above all else and that we will continue to evaluate the situation and keep them informed of the immediate steps taken towards their safety. Leaders should ensure that their team knows they are constantly looking around them for opportunities in improving their welfare and trying to make the best decisions for the team.

Leaders sometimes find themselves in situations where decisions might not unfold as expected. The COVID-19 pandemic serves as a stark reminder of this truth. It was a delicate balance between waiting for complete information and making timely choices, knowing that delay might cost more than imperfection.

From my vantage point, effective leadership is like weaving a web of communication, regardless of whether times are tranquil or tumultuous.

The emphasis on connection and dialogue takes centre stage and where egos need to be set aside, paving the way for collaborative strength to shine.

Throughout moments of crisis, clarity is a lifeline. Leaders must stand as beacons of concise, unwavering messages, adjusting their course if the impact is not as anticipated. It is intriguing to see how relationships nurtured during calming moments can become invaluable assets when chaos descends.

For me, leadership is akin to harnessing the sum of strengths within a team. It is about kindling inspiration and support while embracing the tenacity that bolsters vulnerability. True leadership lies in the art of humility, where gratitude is openly expressed, and appreciation is woven into the fabric of interactions.

In the realm of decision-making, I have found that a blend of confidence and determination is pivotal. Leaders are architects of direction, unafraid to take risks and stand by their choices. They hold the rudder with unwavering hands, guiding the ship towards the intended horizon.

In this journey, impartiality becomes a cornerstone. Leadership thrives in an environment of high objectivity, free from unconscious bias. It is a stance that ensures fair management and balanced decisions.

The web of leadership I have adopted is one that values connection, collaboration, trust, and clarity. It thrives on the strength of diverse talents I uplifted and nurtured within my team, relies on the courage to navigate the unknown, and embraces the humility that sparks genuine bonds. I have come to embrace leadership as a dynamic environment that nurtures growth and propels progress.

When the world is falling apart, leading with confidence requires acknowledging the uncertainty but giving assurance that the team will conquer any problems together.

"US" and Our Emotions in Times of Crisis

The psychological toll of traumatic events impacts not only you, but also those close to you and the people you lead. When situations become out of your control, it is natural to suffer symptoms of depression and frustration; however, it is vital to prioritize your own well-being before you can oversee others. As I outlined previously, remember the airline attendant's words of wisdom: get your oxygen mask on before helping anyone else.

Here are some methods to take care of yourself, the "ME" emotions: Recognize that you aren't a superhero and that you require additional mental fitness to adapt to your specific situation. Once you are able, strive to maintain a regular schedule; this will give you more confidence and return you to a state of normalcy. Maintain your daily regimen with a well-balanced diet and regularly planned meals. Resist the urge to use drugs or alcohol as a kind of escapism, as this tends to increase long-term feelings of despair. Make sure you have like-minded, positive, and loving people who support you and are available for you to consult, reflect, and share ideas toward mutual goals. Share and express your emotions with the correct support since it can bring significant perspective and aid. Keep notes and emails with your personal thoughts and emotions, as this can allow you take stock and use your "me time" to reflect on your personal and team progress as you pass through some difficult moments.

Aside from taking care of oneself, it is critical to take care of others. Here are some recommendations for taking care of "US"—your team—when emotions are still fresh on the surface. Make yourself available to listen. Assure them that we are all secure. Help with domestic responsibilities such as shopping, cleaning, cooking, or childcare, and consider scheduling group transportation and outings to shop and participate in group activities. Spend time with "THEM." Encourage them to get lots of rest and eat healthy. Make sure they have some alone time. Recognize their anguish and encourage and support their ability to cope. Make sure they have other support systems and/or networks in their lives. Assist them in recognizing when it is time to seek outside assistance. You may ignite your team's internal motivation and develop a resilient work environment by applying these strategies.

"US" Managing Meetings

During a crisis, meetings may be less important than other forms of communication and action. With current technological advancements, you and your team members can now utilize various communication channels, such as emails, instant messaging, and videoconferencing, to exchange vital information and make decisions. Whatever system you and your team decide to use, make sure not to change this agreed-upon channel. This will only add more confusion for all. In our case, we used our own Facebook group as one rally point but also used other channels between team leaders. It is essential to focus on taking action to address the situation rather than spending too much time discussing it. Meetings can sometimes create a false sense of progress or complacency when the most critical work is being done outside of the meeting.

While meetings are sometimes necessary, such as when decisions must be made by a group or when face-to-face communication is required, it is critical to weigh the benefits of holding a meeting against the potential drawbacks. Time is of the essence, and there may be a sense of urgency and a need for quick decision-making. Meetings can sometimes slow down the decision-making process, as people may spend too much time discussing or debating ideas instead of acting.

Meetings are still important during a crisis, and communication and coordination is required. Hold structured, informative, and timely meetings with the right people to oversee each stage of the crisis. Selecting individuals whose expertise are relevant at a particular time during the crisis is also beneficial.

To make meetings more productive and focused, have everyone who is able, to stand rather than sit, especially for operational meetings that include routine topics and feedback, which are known as "stand-up" meetings. This format encourages everyone to be more accountable, relevant, and precise, with a sense of urgency, as ad hoc strategies and initiatives are managed. Allow chairs to be pulled back for strategic meetings, and submit a proposed agenda ahead of time, asking for feedback on the themes to be discussed; for operational meetings, use a repeating agenda format that is brief and concise, with feedback from those involved.

When striving for long-term survival, individuals should connect their personal goals to a clear, overarching purpose that can be broken down into specific activities. During these strategic meetings, you must "plan your work and work your plan."[30] To ensure sustained success for your group, it is essential to harmonize individual aspirations with a clearly outlined overarching aim. This central goal ought to be laid out in clear actionable steps, enabling steady advancement toward the desired outcomes. As the leader you play a pivotal role in keeping the team steadfast towards these objectives.

During times of crisis, careful planning and effective communication are necessary to organize phone and video meetings, ensuring the sharing of valuable information and decision-making tasks.

Efficient communication ensures that teams stay connected. For a regular face-to-face meeting, ensure that you send an agenda in a timely manner to clearly define the purpose of the meeting and specify the specific issues or challenges that need to be addressed. Choose a reliable video conferencing platform or phone conferencing service. Ensure that all participants have access to and are familiar with the chosen technology. Additionally, it is important to establish clear guidelines for participation and etiquette during the meeting, such as muting microphones when not speaking and raising hands to indicate a desire to speak. This will help maintain order and prevent interruptions. Finally, designate a facilitator

---

30   Napoleon Hill, "Plan Your Work and Work Your Plan," accessed on January 21, 2024, https://quotefancy.com/quote/871599/ Napoleon-Hill-Plan-your-work-and-work-your-plan.

or moderator to keep the meeting on track and ensure that all participants have an opportunity to contribute their thoughts and ideas.

Make sure everyone is properly introduced and know what their roles are within your emergency response team. Assign roles such as a facilitator, timekeeper, and note-taker, to ensure a smooth flow and record key points. Encourage active participation from all attendees, but also establish ground rules to maintain order. Keep the meeting focused on the pre-defined objectives and agenda items. Manage time effectively to ensure all topics are addressed.

Foster a supportive and empathetic atmosphere where participants feel comfortable sharing their thoughts and concerns. Encourage open and honest communication and be prepared to address any emotional reactions or stress.

After the meeting, distribute meeting minutes or a summary of key points and action items. Set deadlines and expectations for follow-up actions. Schedule a follow-up meeting if necessary to track progress. Be prepared to adapt your meeting schedule and approach as the crisis evolves. Flexibility is crucial in dynamic situations.

To avoid mentally "injuring" team members who may struggle in uncertain situations, leaders must address vulnerabilities, focus on harm reduction, and implement damage control measures. This can be facilitated through role-playing, "as-if" exercises, and assigned mental tasks that allow team members to articulate thoughts and emotions that they may otherwise not articulate.

"US" Applying the Ten Commandments of Crisis Leadership

Personal Log: Edmonton, Alberta, May 5 to May 18, 2016: Through Hell!

On the morning of May 5, we joined part of our team at the Hilton Garden Inn in Edmonton, a property managed by Atlific through the expertise of George Marine who was previously part of Team WOne in Fort McMurray. My wife, our puppy Jaxx, and I were exhausted, and we collapsed for a few hours to catch some sleep and clean up, as our clothes stank of smoke. Soon after, the cell phone rang constantly, and I had to organize the team for what would be a few weeks, with no idea of the situation in Fort McMurray, if we could come back, or what we would find when we returned.

I focused on the immediate and listened to the initial feedback from the field. Everyone was in good spirits, but their primary concerns were if they would still get paid while being evacuated. Once the sense of urgency had settled, I addressed this issue, which was quickly resolved thanks to the ownership and management company's commitment and support in helping us through this difficult period.

I had multiple calls with Robert Chartrand, CEO of Atlific, who mobilized the entire resources of the company from payroll to IT, legal, and supplies, among others, at his disposal. In addition, help came from the provincial government's temporary subsidies and the Red Cross, among many others. Strangers came to wherever our team and families were staying and dropped off clothes, food, and various supplies. Feeling powerless against the magnitude of Mother Nature's rage, this gave us all a sense of optimism, which helped us over this period of uncertainties.

Two days later, I was on a conference call with some of Fort McMurray's city councillors, business leaders, and the emergency centre based in Fort McMurray, giving us much-welcomed news confirming that the Beast was under control. Our properties would be the first to move back to get basic population needs operational, such as grocery stores, banks, gas stations, and hospital doctors, nurses, and other services. This was most encouraging, but I knew the planning to get us all back would take lots of coordination. At least I had a goal and a vision to get us back and had to work on a plan to execute our re-entry.

In the meantime, our displaced team, family, and pets settled in, and we organized activities to keep the morale up. Robert Chartrand escorted by Gill Vallee, General Manager of the Sheraton Red Deer flew from Montreal to visit all the displaced employees and families dispersed through our Alberta properties all the way down to Lake Louise Inn where the usual most hospitable Nuwan Eparatchy accommodated some of our displaced team members, family, and pets. Robert's action gave us all a boost, and it reassured us of the tremendous support and extraordinary understanding the entire company had for us.

The way you conduct yourself during a crisis will influence how your peers perceive your crisis management abilities, not only during the crisis, but long after it. Although there are countless do's and don'ts in times of crisis, if I were to create a brief list of essential actions to guide me through such situations, I would include:

1. Prioritize the most key facts and be selective in your data collection.

2. Before action, carefully weigh your options, but do not let indecision hold you back.

3. Delegate duties to foster a culture of empowerment and trust among your team.

4. Encourage open dialogue, seek independent thought, and respect input and ideas from others.

5. Keep a cheerful outlook while remaining realistic.

6. Use checklists to help you regulate and prioritize your decision-making.

7. Maintain your agility and adaptability in the face of new developments.

8. Maintain a thorough awareness of all information, roles, and directions communicated within your organization.

9. Take care of yourself by practising healthy behaviours and controlling your emotions and tone of voice.

10. Be available for self-reflection and introspection to keep control over your emotions and personal well-being.

What is an effective team, and how can you lead one during a crisis? Teams are complex entities within organizations, and operating across different time zones and countries can present communication challenges. During a crisis, the leader must amplify the competencies of team members and accept responsibility for potential failures in crisis management.

The team's environment. Who surrounds you? Internal and external teams, resources, specialists, consultants, reaction teams. Avoid teams functioning in silos; build relationships and share information from the start of a crisis.

The structure of the team. During a crisis, there is a propensity to hope for the best, but having a structured environment can give stability and prevent counterproductive behaviours from team leaders.

Communication and respect for each other's roles and responsibilities are paramount for team effectiveness. Basic rules for forming effective teams include having the right team size, complementary skills, well-defined goals, an agreed approach to working together, and a sense of mutual accountability.

To avoid chaos and assure success, effective team leadership needs to give attention to the team's environment, structure, and coherence.

As a leader of leaders, you must manage new and ever-changing objectives with little time to react. Fortunately, minor expenditures in support and coaching can increase your leaders' performance during a crisis. When the immediate chaos subsides and you find a moment to reflect, take note of those who rose to the occasion and those who faced challenges, and analyze the reasons behind their responses. Also, consider how roles may evolve in the post-crisis world and whether your key executives are well-positioned for success.

"US" and Learning to Better Communicate Internally During Crisis

In the next part of this book, I elaborate on the leadership tasks during a crisis. A certain resemblance to a military environment is welcome in times of crisis since the military has centuries of experience and practices executed by disciplined leaders around the world and throughout history.

To be an effective crisis leader, you must maintain a constant sense of command and control while balancing an autocratic and authoritarian style with keen listening skills. Decisiveness is essential, and during a crisis, the commanding leadership style is the most appropriate. However, finding the right balance is critical because a leader must be task-oriented while avoiding the trap of self-demagoguery, which could lead to low morale and a broken spirit within the team.

Your team will closely observe and interpret your body language, tone of voice, and actions. Remember: your team will initially react to the situation in the same way as you. These first moments will determine whether your team feels safe following your guidance and whether they will work as a team, rather than only focusing on their individual needs.

When communicating, try to speak calmly and purposefully remembering to control the speed of your words and to breathe between moments. The "fire-panel" amygdala may still ring, and your adrenaline will pump, so it is important to stay focused. Allow for a brief open-floor session before moving on with the initial phases.

Schedule subsequent calls with enough notice for everyone to attend and ensure that the group does not veer off topic. Focus on relevant data and information for the current tone and urgencies of the meeting. Ensure that the team understands the big picture and that you cascade various roles and responsibilities as you progress through the crisis.

Use language that conveys confidence and unity, such as "I propose" or "Based on the information I am given, I suggest . . .." Avoid dictatorial language, such as "I demand" or "I want." Use "we" as frequently as possible to demonstrate that the team works together.

Remind everyone to be sensitive in their daily interactions with others, as people are on edge. Be honest and truthful in your public comments, and recognize the fact that people want to matter during times of uncertainty. Ensure that you are available to your team but acknowledge that you may not have all the answers they want to hear and that it may take time to find solutions.

After each call or meeting, repeat the high-level expectations for clarity and do not forget to thank everyone and their families for their efforts during these challenging times. Let everyone know when the next call or meeting will be and try to establish a regular schedule as soon as possible to provide a sense of normalcy and rhythm in their lives.

Remember to separate frequently scheduled operational meetings from less frequent strategic meetings, allowing time in between.

"US" in between Meetings

Having someone designated to take minutes during a group call or meeting is always helpful as it allows the group to refer to previous decisions and ensure clarity when needed.

In his highly insightful book *Team of Teams: New Rules of Engagement for a Complex World*, author General Stanley McChrystal, with Tantum Collins, David Silverman, and Chris Fussell, draws attention to a common oversight made by team leaders. Rather than merely assigning a task to a team, he emphasizes the importance of clarifying the steps needed to solve a problem.[31]

This can be likened to a football game where the goal post is a well-known objective, yet the challenge lies in effectively navigating the path to reach it. Especially when dealing with senior members of the leadership team, articulating the actionable steps towards achieving goals becomes crucial.

General McChrystal advocates for a culture of open dialogue by encouraging leaders to "think aloud" and openly share the current collective thought process. It becomes evident that decision-making is a collaborative effort rather than an individual endeavour. This approach fosters an environment of inclusivity and allows room for mutual understanding, further discussions, and necessary corrections.

Remind everyone that you are available 24/7, to the best of your abilities. You must be available to the main stakeholders, some of whom may be in different time zones, and they need to be informed of your progress and challenges. This obligation forces you to make sure you allow yourself some "me time," a critical discipline you must gain from the start.

Just like Formula 1 drivers take a walk through the entire course ahead of their qualifying rounds, leaders going through a crisis must visualize themselves overcoming the challenges. Visualization is key to self-confidence.

Subsequent meetings should follow the same principles, focusing less on the how and more on the what and who. You can then extend limited participation or input by inviting guests with specialized expertise capable of assisting the group, saving you time trying to explain yourself to a particular task using external resources.

The suggestions above are not required, but they are useful tools to assist you through what will be difficult moments for everyone involved. In the end, during a crisis, you must demonstrate urgent control of yourself while constantly improving a collaborative approach.

---

31   Graham Mann, "Team of Teams: New Rules of Engagement for a Complex World by General Stanley McChrystal: Summary & Notes," GrahamMann.net, accessed November 11, 2023, https://www.grahammann.net/book-notes/team-of-teams-general-stanley-mcchrystal.

"US" Practising the Four P's in a Crisis

During my career in the hotel industry, I gained significant insight into the importance of the four P's in sales and marketing: product, people, pricing, and place of distribution. In times of crisis, the four P's take on a different meaning.

People. People are the most important "P" during a crisis. One practice I implemented in our hotel portfolio was promoting from within. We provided coaching and career development opportunities to our front office clerks, and some eventually became front office managers. A few even rose to the position of hotel general manager. When I retired, I entrusted this critical role to someone who started as a night auditor and eventually became an area director, climbing the necessary steps towards taking this significant role. In the last few years I was in this role, I stepped back from day-to-day operational duties and execution to focus on being a teacher, which allowed me to help future leaders gain confidence and knowledge while permeating throughout the entire organization. Having a cross-trained "bullpen" of future leaders will provide your organization with a solid foundation. As a leader, it is your responsibility to mentor and coach the next generation, as it is your legacy on which you are working. While they may forget your personal success, they will never forget how you taught them.

Process. It is tempting to micromanage to assure the survival of your firm; nevertheless, micromanagement does not benefit anyone. It is time-consuming for you and disheartening for your personnel. Reduce the desire to micromanage by implementing the right tools and processes. Create standard operating procedures (SOPs) that outline how to run specific areas of your organization during a crisis. Determine tasks you can only do, other leaders can do, and even what the business owner can help you with. Then create procedures for each department or unit. When faced with a crisis, it is beneficial to challenge the standards that were created in a safe office or training environment, as the standard may be confusing or even not applicable. It is not the time to take shortcuts in your processes. This could have disastrous consequences. As you follow processes, there is always room for improvement or to leave some room for innovation and invention, but you must convey these improvements, which should have been collectively agreed by all parties.

Patience. It may be the art of waiting without complaining, but in times of crisis, patience takes on a greater significance. It is the ability to remain calm in the face of adversity, frustration, or suffering. It is important to consider how we respond, and patience, like a muscle, requires commitment and practice to develop.

It is also necessary to practise compassion and appreciate all efforts and acts performed by others. The most critical issues must be prioritized, as unexpected events may develop, necessitating swift adaptation.

Patience, compassion, and resilience are important qualities to have during a crisis, and while developing these qualities might be difficult, it is attainable with practice and determination.

Proactivity. Being pro-active involves anticipating potential challenges, identifying opportunities, and taking pre-emptive action to address them before they escalate. It requires staying ahead of the curve, continually monitoring the situation, and adjusting strategies accordingly. It also involves fostering a culture of preparedness within the organization, where individuals are empowered to take initiative and adapt to changing circumstances swiftly.

When a crisis presents adversity, use it as a performance-enhancing drug, accepting the situation and catalyzing learning and growth, which may include developing new systems, processes, and policies; improving interpersonal relationships and communication; and laying a foundation of trust that supports greater resilience in navigating complex adversities.

Personal Reflections on "US"

In the first hour of each crisis, I immediately recognized how important my closest team of leaders would be to myself and everyone else. I understood that leveraging their individual talents and expertise would be critical.

Establishing a system of communication and feedback was essential for coordinating and sharing information as events rapidly unfolded. I had to be cautious not to overwhelm them with duties and tasks, especially considering many of them were dealing with the devastating loss of shelters. Providing support while also expecting a certain level of accountability for immediate recovery tasks was a delicate balance.

Having developed a closely knit group of leaders, each with their own expertise and personalities, I then focused on harnessing their individual talents for mutual benefit. In the initial hours of the crisis and even as we worked towards re-entry into town weeks later, each leader contributed their unique insights, skills, and perspectives. I did not hesitate to tap into their knowledge during these challenging times, which further solidified the elevated level of trust I had in them. Once I assigned them their specific tasks and directives, which we had agreed to pursue, I had complete confidence that they would not only achieve the intended results but surpass them. As General George Patton wisely reminds us: "Never tell people how to do things. Tell them what to do and they will surprise you with ingenuity."

From the very beginning, one of my primary goals was to hire the best individuals I believed could be moulded into an effective group. I shared with them a vision that we all wholeheartedly embraced, allowing them to operate within their individual environments. Regular communication about their progress, challenges, and outcomes was crucial. I believe the solid foundations of trust we all adhered, and practiced, paid significant benefits for us all.

During these crises, I often wished for more time to personally meet with all my team members scattered across Alberta; however, through my leadership team, I ensured they had access to the resources needed to care for themselves, their families, and their pets. This became one of my top priorities.

Coordinating and following up on the various programs we implemented, demanded a sizeable portion of my time, but both my leaders and I understood the importance of continually instilling hope. The psychological impact of these crises was unknown, particularly after the evacuation of an entire city due to wildfires. I worried that some team members, having lost their homes and belongings, might lose their determination, and quit. Remarkably, 98 percent of our labour force returned and began rebuilding their lives. We knew that by supporting each other, we could navigate the challenges that lay ahead, including subsequent floods, a pandemic, and economic downturns.

A few months after our return following the wildfires and once, we had stabilized as much as possible, the team organized a gathering to celebrate our collective achievements over the tumultuous past months. Frames with blank canvas pieces were obtained, and team members dipped and imprinted their hands in various paint colours, symbolizing our unity and resilience. One team member painted a message that resonated deeply with me: "The Beast took my home, but it did not take my spirit."

PART THREE:
"THEM" THOUGH HELL
AND HIGH WATER

"THEM" and Survival of the Fittest

We endured the initial month of the COVID-19 pandemic, coping with the constantly changing strategies that the world was implementing to combat this devastating virus. Our team took immediate measures to prevent any infections within our ranks. Our earlier challenges were getting enough personal protective equipment (PPE) while navigating through the constant instructions from municipal, provincial, and federal governmental entities and agencies. Despite these trying times, the team worked diligently and communicated effectively to ensure their safety and the safety of our guests. As if this were not enough to deal with, Mother Nature had other challenges for us.

Personal Log: Fort McMurray, Alberta, April 26, 2020: Through High Water!

April 26, 2020, 10:00 a.m. to 2:00 p.m.: High Water

Fort McMurray is at the confluence of three rivers: the Athabasca, Clearwater, and Hangingstone. In past years, the town has experienced floods caused by a surge in water flow through these rivers.

I was on my prime property, the Clearwater Suite Hotel downtown, listening to local news and reading various comments on the situation. The situation was becoming more worrisome by the hour since an ice jam further up the river was blocking any water flow. The porous berm system allowed water to gush into our community.

According to the CBC article "Berms and Sandbags: Fort McMurray Spending Millions in Preparation for Flood Season," *"Water passed* *over parts of the berms that were too low to withstand a one-in-one-hundred-year flood, pouring into downtown through culverts and vents that run through the berms, causing more than $520 million in insured damage.*[32]

Here we go again!

It was time to lead another crisis on top of the pandemic crisis we were already facing! Once again, we mobilized the same basic communication system through our Facebook group page to monitor which of our team members would be affected. Mandatory evacuation was confined to the core of downtown. The most affected area was south of the rivers, in the area ominously called Waterways. That area had already been devastated by the wildfires of 2016 and was now flooded, causing severe physical damage and mental distress for citizens who had persevered to rebuild after the fires. They now had to pack for survival. The balance of the day was once again focused on relocating our team members, who had lost their homes, to some of our other properties not affected by the downtown area.

April 26, 2020, 4:00 p.m. to 8:00 p.m.: High Water

All our downtown properties were under mandatory evacuation. The water had slowly gained ground, cutting downtown into two-thirds, with some areas completely submerged at high-water levels and moderate flooding in the last third of downtown. The team was familiar with following the same instructions, advising incoming and outgoing guests, and securing the property.

Once again, I made sure I was the last one leaving the downtown properties, leaving one security guard to sleep on the highest level of our property with specific instructions to monitor the situation and call me if he saw the water reaching the property. I was confident

---

32 Jamie Malbeuf, "Berms and sandbags: Fort McMurray spending millions in preparation for flood season," CBC News, March 2021, https://www.cbc.ca/news/canada/edmonton/fort-mcmurray-flood-river-wood-buffalo-1.5956024#:~:text=The%20municipality%20has%20spent%20%2410,to%20be%20completed%20this%20year.

that the water flow would subside but did not expect the city culverts to overflow and embarrass most of the downtown sewer system.

This recent crisis demanded once again that we dig deep within our-selves to find the will to climb a steep hill and stay afloat. I believe, we call this "resilience."

Our internal compass directs us to first understand ourselves, allowing us to appraise our capabilities while encouraging internal communication with the "US" within our business. This emphasis on the team that sur-rounds "ME" is critical. Strong teams focus not only on the operational components of crisis management but also on the well-being of affected individuals and communities outside of their own. They provide support, guidance, and resources to people who have been directly impacted, guaranteeing their safety, access to critical services, and timely recov-ery assistance.

Animals are fascinating, as certain species have survived despite all odds, whereas people have made their lives so tough that they have died in droves. Many animal species have survival instincts and intuition from which we can learn. During long-distance flights, for example, Canadian geese follow a consistent, shared set of leadership rotation duties, a habit hard-wired into their DNA. Ants, termites, and bees, all work together and collaborate for survival. In a crisis, no leader can act alone; and as humans we must collaborate with various organizations and entities that can help or obstruct our desired development for survival.

Leading in a crisis necessitates military discipline due to the numerous elements and inputs. When a crisis happens, several performers appear on the stage, including victims, heroes, and the media in-between acting as narrators. There is often finger-pointing and second-guessing after a catastrophe, with the finger-pointing dance replicating the best of a Bolshoi Ballet.

Internal and external teams must be considered, with each one contrib-uting to the resources required to solve problems. Unfortunately, various teams may have separate goals and priorities that do not always coincide. In *Team of Teams*, General Stanley McChrystal's Team addresses this, discussing the "silo" effect, which occurs when teams work individually toward the same goal, making the process more complex. He challenged his troops with a clear sense of collective purpose, emphasizing the importance and interdependence of all teams.

All leaders must prioritize the development of external relationships. During my time as area director for this hotel group, I made a point to constantly know and maintain good relationships with the major players in the local community. This was a deliberate and strategic approach that included participation in numerous tourism committees and organizations, the local chamber of commerce, economic and downtown redevelopment programs, and similar community engagements. I participated in strategic sessions and was visible in relevant forums, listening to professionals in their disciplines and developing business ties across a broad spectrum of interests.

During corporate visits to our city, we went to several venues and met numerous people. I was frequently asked, "Do you know everyone here?" Of course, I did not know everyone in the market, but I developed good relationships with those who were most important to my work. Regular lunches, activities, and business meetings all provided opportunities to build these bonds.

These efforts paid off handsomely when I needed support, assistance, or information during a crisis or elsewhere. Our town is small in comparison to larger urban regions, but I highly advise all leaders to connect within their own circles. Building ties with people who are willing and able to assist can be quite beneficial during tough times.

Personal Log: Fort McMurray, Alberta, May to June 2020: Through High Water!

We found ourselves amid two major crises: the floods and COVID-19. The city had called on me to assist with the downtown residents who had lost their homes, some of whom had unfortunately experienced this tragedy twice in just four years. The city requested that we provide accommodation for entire families who were displaced and disoriented, some of whom were losing hope.

I had to navigate this terrible situation while my team still grappled with the uncertainties and dangers of COVID-19. The new safety regulations encroached on our guests' usual comfort and rules of hospitality. I had to rely on the dedication, loyalty, and determination of my leaders and teams to carefully balance the needs of our concerned, displaced guests while remaining sensitive to the morale and state of mind of the team and maintaining constant adaptive strategies. I can humbly say that if we did not invent the word "pivot," we came close to it.

Once again, our relationships with the city administration, the Red Cross, the provincial and municipal governments, and others helped us act and react quickly to the demands imposed by these two simultaneous crises. My focus was, as always, to ensure the safety of our team and guests. I was now reporting to our new VP, Mr. Gordon Johnson, and with his support and the management company's corporate office, we could get an initial stock of PPE supplies while I was learning every hour of the simultaneous developments happening on both fronts of these two crises.

"THEM" and the Security Blanket

In the previous chapters, you have already met my puppy dog Jaxx, who has a rag doll nicknamed his snake that he runs to when he is stressed.

We frequently face internal conflicts during times of uncertainty because we are overwhelmed with a barrage of information, rumours, unverified truths, advice, views, and other inputs. Some of this information may be presented in good faith, while others may be misguided accidentally due to a lack of education or comprehensive research.

It is natural to feel pressured to know what is coming ahead and to be ready for any surprises. This yearning for comfort in known facts results in the formation of a mental security blanket. The more information we have, such as facts and data, the better equipped we are to deal with pressure and emergencies.

When we lack all the information we require, we must be tenacious in our pursuit of proper knowledge. We must investigate all possibilities until we are pleased with the results. We should also think outside of the box and examine different scenarios and actions we can take while speaking with our trusted team leaders. To interpret the large amount of information we face, we must employ the appropriate filters.

We must avoid becoming closed-minded and remain open to new alternatives. Even though people have comparable backgrounds, they may have different viewpoints and interpretations of the scenario. We should challenge and encourage debate, compare diverse points of view, and strive for a blended and balanced approach that considers all known facts. While internal conflict and polarized ideas are unavoidable, team trust and respect can encourage healthy and constructive discussions. We should not be afraid of productive disputes because they can lead to faster problem resolution.

We must agree on a clear course and properly express our aims and plans to all parties concerned. In times like these, where everything seems uncertain and chaotic, mental security blankets, something that comforts us and gives us a sense of stability. For me, that was the dedication and commitment of my team and the unwavering support of our partners which helped me in overcoming the challenges and support of those in need.

"THEM" Thinking and Acting as a Marine

Today's corporate leaders confronting various crises can seek advice from military commanders. Military leaders have faced major obstacles throughout history, and managing through complicated situations today can often feel like being engulfed in the uncertainties of war. Learning from the experience of highly competent military leaders can be beneficial. I offered a few examples of such historical conditions earlier in this book but let me give a few more examples that I particularly love, and feel are pertinent to the fundamental components of managing various crises.

In the realm of navigating tough challenges, today's business executives can draw valuable insights from a fundamental principle often seen in the military: the power of decisiveness. For example, during Napoleon's invasion of Russia in 1812, the esteemed Russian Field Marshal Mikhail Kutuzov faced a pivotal choice. He made the bold decision to relinquish Moscow to the invading French forces. This strategic move, although painful, allowed him to regroup and eventually confront Napoleon from a position of renewed strength, leading to a triumphant outcome.

Do not wallow in your defeats; instead, rebuild your company and regroup to fight from a position of strength. Exceptional military leaders have consistently displayed a firsthand approach, actively engaging in combat alongside their troops. Napoleon's very presence on the battlefield, as observed by the Duke of Wellington, wielded an influence akin to an additional forty thousand soldiers.[33] While Napoleon's reputation was built on meticulous planning and effective time management, it was Wellington's dynamic troop movements and agile repositioning of armies that led to his victory over Napoleon at Waterloo.

A cornerstone of effective leadership lies in fostering confidence, especially during crises like a pandemic. During such challenging times, when the well-being of workers and their families takes precedence, military leaders understand the paramount importance of exuding unwavering assurance and optimism. This unwavering demeanour has been a cornerstone of successful military commanders throughout history. It is a testament to their ability to inspire and guide, even amid the gravest of circumstances, ensuring that their troops remain steadfast and focused on the path ahead. For example, at Agincourt, Henry V effectively used his troops' mobility and ferocity to his advantage. By seizing openings and upsetting French army formations, Henry V exhibited amazing confidence, increased morale, and encouraged his troops to face an adversary three times their size rather than withdrawing as other commanders may have done. Inspiring and encouraging soldiers requires effective communication.

Winston Churchill, known for his resolute leadership, challenged bureaucratic norms by prioritizing actions marked "Action this Day," thereby instilling accountability within his generals. Churchill utilized the power of words to mobilize his troops for battle, whereas Napoleon often sent encouraging messages to his troops. Excessive communication, on the other hand, can cause confusion, as seen during the Vietnam War when the United States military swamped inboxes with lengthy and urgent communiqués.

In my journey of leadership, I have found that military leaders often champion the values of agility and effective decision-making. They reward those who demonstrate successful command with increased responsibilities and swift advancements. During moments of crisis, the unique needs of various levels within an organization come to the forefront. It is a

---

33   Andrew Knighton, "7 Ways Napoleon Celebrated Battlefield Courage, "War History On Line", February 14, 2016, https://www.warhistoryonline.com/napoleon/7-ways-napoleon-celebrated-battlefield-courage.html

dynamic puzzle where struggling leaders receive gradual guidance and a reduction in responsibilities until they find their stride.

Just like soldiers require rest, sustenance, and moments of leisure, so do the gears of any organization need their nourishment. I am reminded of General Washington's strategic choice during the Revolutionary War. Instead of yielding to political pressures for an immediate offensive against British forces in Philadelphia, he opted to station his troops in Valley Forge. This decision not only allowed his troops to regroup and recharge, but it also underscored the importance of strategy rooted in understanding the unique rhythms of a team.

As we navigate the intricate path of reopening workplaces, bolstering our businesses, and rekindling team spirit, it is crucial to glean wisdom from past crises. A fresh management approach beckons, characterized by resolute decision-making, close collaboration with employees, the nimbleness of agility, the warmth of optimism, the art of inspiring communication, and the embrace of flexibility.

Nonetheless, it's critical to remember Eisenhower's adage: "Plans are nothing; planning is everything."[34] This expresses the idea that the process is important in relation to the outcome, emphasizing the importance of precise preparation in successful leadership.

I frequently refer to the US Marine Corps's unofficial slogan of improvise, adapt, and overcome. Although I have no military background, I have educated myself on various systems and processes, and I have avidly read a good deal of leadership books detailing generals and low-level grunts in military operations going through battle and ongoing crises.

While there are numerous models to pick from, I will highlight a few that have some overlap and are still useful. After the Cold War, the US Army War College introduced the VUCA method. VUCA stands for volatility, uncertainty, complexity, and ambiguity. This was coined to describe the world's rising complexity because of a variety of circumstances.[35] It has since found use in the corporate arena, as VUCA accurately

---

34 General Dwight D. Eisenhower, Brainy Quotes, accessed January 23, 2024, https://www.brainyquote.com/quotes/dwight_d_eisenhower_149111.

35 "VUCA," Wikipedia, last modified November 10, 2023, https://en.wikipedia.org/wiki/VUCA.

portrays the issues that firms face in today's landscape. Navigating foreign markets, managing constant restructuring, reacting to growth, or downsizing, responding to economic and global impacts, embracing technical breakthroughs, adapting to cultural and societal shifts, and much more are among these obstacles.

VUCA leadership principles are intended to help leaders navigate the fast-paced and unpredictable changes that have become the new normal in today's modern world. This leadership strategy recognizes the necessity to confront volatile, uncertain, complicated, and ambiguous circumstances and contexts.

Volatility is defined by frequent and fast changes.

Uncertainty refers to the unpredictability of events.

Complexity emphasizes the numerous aspects and issues to be considered.

Ambiguity highlights the fact that there is a lack of clarity, understanding, and precision because of the many meanings and messages inside a scenario.

VUCA can be used as a framework for managing a specific crisis since it provides a process. I am all about procedures because they force me to have mental discipline to execute in trying times. Navigating this environment successfully necessitates dissecting VUCA into its parts and identifying circumstances that exhibit volatility, uncertainty, complexity, or ambiguity. Each sort of issue has its own set of reasons and answers, so focus on one at a time.

Recognize and embrace change as a natural and unpredictable part of your crisis environment rather than resisting it. There is no need to mourn over spilled milk.

Create a clear, shared vision of the immediate future after you have produced a powerful, compelling, and cohesive declaration of team aims and values.

Set customizable goals for your team members that may be changed as needed. This allows them to navigate through unpredictable and unfamiliar situations and respond quickly to unforeseen developments that may occur without warning.

When faced with uncertainty, pay attention to the mood of your immediate leaders, and observe your surroundings. This can assist you in comprehending and developing new ways of thinking and acting in response to volatility, uncertainty, complexity, and ambiguity.

Determine what you know and what you do not know. Prioritize investing in, analyzing, and understanding information and competitive intelligence to avoid falling behind.

Keep abreast of internal and external changes and pay close attention to all constituencies and constituents but be selective in who you choose to listen to.

Examine your decisions both alone and with your emergency response team. Consider what you did well, what surprised you, and where you may improve.

Begin with the result and work your way backward. Sync skills, accept and capitalize on behaviours and reactions, and transform fear and resistance into positive energy. Simulate and experiment with various scenarios to see how they might play out.

Attempt to anticipate potential future hazards and prepare responses. Recognize and make transparent interconnections. When confronted with complexity, speak clearly with your team. In demanding situations, clear, defined communication helps them comprehend the direction of your team or company.

Cascade information and maintain mobility within your internal organization. Create teams and encourage everyone to work together. Simplicity is essential. Focus on the key elements that genuinely matter. Direct your energy and efforts where they will have the most impact. Encourage flexibility, adaptability, and agility to combat ambiguity. Plan ahead of time but allow for contingencies and be prepared to change your plans as fast-changing events occur.

Surround yourself with people who thrive in VUCA situations. These people are often collaborative, comfortable with ambiguity and change, and have high critical-thinking skills.

Create a collaborative environment and strive hard to reach an agreement. Encourage everyone to participate in debate, disagreement, and involvement. In unpredictable times, embrace a "trust culture" that can give your company a creative and nimble edge.

Another military concept is the OODA loop. United States Air Force Colonel John Boyd conceived this under the acronyms of observe, orient, determine, and act.[36] Boyd had a profound knowledge of leading under pressure, and his approach may assist leaders in problem-solving under pressure, making decisions in times of ambiguity, and instilling confidence in their team.

To use the OODA loop, first become aware of what is going on and remain calm. Then analyze your situation, decide what you are going to do about it, and trust your instincts. Act on your decisions, evaluate the outcomes, and repeat the process. You can successfully manage the hurdles of crisis circumstances and lead your team to a brighter future by adopting these tactics. You can also create your own procedure. I highly advise leaders going through a significant crisis to adapt to their specific conditions, as each crisis has its own distinct traits and patterns.

Following a VUCA or OODA structure to the letter may cause leaders to lose focus on the current situation. While these frameworks give a straight and logical path, they are processes that must be customized to the situation. They provide a framework for leaders to mobilize their groups around a clear direction and refocus, which is especially important because lesser crises are frequently contained within larger crises.

My colleagues and I were in the second month of dealing with the coronavirus pandemic in June 2020. We had to adjust swiftly, like the rest of the globe, to safeguard ourselves, our team, and our guests. Although COVID-19 had a lower level of emergency than the citywide evacuation we had to conduct after the May 2016 wildfires, I rapidly evaluated the limits of the VUCA and OODA frameworks and developed our own model to manage the issue.

We had to deal with the aftermath of recent floods, which had a significant impact on some of our assets as well as the well-being of our team members who had lost their homes. Despite the unknowns of the virus and Mother Nature's wrath, it was critical to transmit a message of positivity to

---

36 "OODA Loop," Wikipedia, last modified September 12, 2023, https://en.wikipedia.org/wiki/OODA_loop.

our staff during this crisis. Using the same premise as acronyms, I designed the BOUNCE program.

The "B" stands for "be us." We focused on who we were as a group, company, and resource in our market. We assessed our strengths and weaknesses to better serve our visitors and staff in these changing conditions. To accomplish this, we revisited Jim Collins's book *Good to Great* and asked ourselves what drives our economic engines, what do we want to be the best at, and what are we currently good at.

The "O" stands for "opportunities." After completing a self-scan in the first phase of BOUNCE, we dug deeper to capitalize on our strengths and identify areas for improvement. We swiftly responded to the ease of electronic communication and established a digital store of current resources for everyone's use. We also looked ahead to see what the future might hold.

The letter "U" stands for "unique," and I challenged our team to differentiate ourselves in how we managed visitor complaints, team morale, and diverse scenarios. Our properties provided food for the flooded families who had been evacuated from their homes.

We used one of our kitchens on one of our properties and built a commissary kitchen that could follow new specific food safety regulations under the "new normal" of COVID 19. We offered different food to certain families because many of them were Muslims and fasted during Ramadan. To do so, I leveraged a local connection I had with a cab owner, who was Muslim, and used his personal relationship with his own mosque kitchen to assist us in serving halal meals to these families according to their *unique* specific dietary requirements. At one of our properties, the general manager, J.D. Girardo played a crucial role in coordinating the catering needs for all concerned.

"N" stands for "nimble." We were always looking for ways to improve our processes and efficiency, accepted technology where it fit our strategy, and pivoted when necessary. We emphasized the necessity of being sensitive while maintaining discipline in our processes to ensure everyone's safety. To effectively manage this problem, we needed to be aware of our team members' mood changes.

Finally, the letter "E" stands for "evaluate," as it was critical to track our progress in implementing our processes and safety measures. We had "champions" appointed to each of our properties to monitor and report any concerns that the team encountered, and they dealt with them quickly. To keep a steady pulse on our company and guests, we established digital infographics, feedback systems, and questionnaires.

This concept started with my own self-imposed "me time" with some hamster biking in our hotel's gym. Following the floods of April 2020, we put mechanisms in place to address the initial realities we faced shortly after everyone was safe and oriented.

While I allocated myself the "vision," Team Wone and all my general managers were assigned a specific portfolio of BOUNCE. We engaged our sales and revenue management department to listen to our guests' expectations under this new normal and to gather the respective opinions of our team members on each property. Because I did not have all the answers, this was a collaborative effort.

During my me time, I needed to filter outside perspectives, resources, and data to comprehend the significance of COVID-19. I had to train myself to tune out and self-reflect since the flow of information, government directives, media releases, and expertise was overwhelming.

Our VP, Gordon Johnson, then implemented this structure at the provincial and regional levels in Western Canada. His assistance as an outside resource was crucial to me since he always presented me with innovative ideas to improve the model at the local and regional levels.

Processes are essential to good crisis management and leadership, whether they are inspired by military methods or created from scratch.

With "THEM," Build Your Own Web of C's

Connections

Leaders must have access to both internal and external resources during a crisis. Building a robust organizational structure, on the other hand, does not happen overnight. When confronted with a crisis, it is critical to have a list of people and resources on hand to help integrate your crisis team structure and offer more positive resources. You cannot manage a crisis on your own. As the issue becomes more complicated by the hour and your regular routine is disturbed, you will rely on not just your closest team leaders but also on outside personnel, agencies, and external resources. Instead, consider crisis management to be operational command and control, and crisis leadership to be the art of persuading people to adapt to change.

Stepping back and studying the scenario to project future actions and then guiding managers to adjust to the originality of the situation is required for effective crisis leadership. Do not become bogged down in detail following a disaster. It is also crucial to establish everyone's job and to acknowledge that not everyone can be a leader during a crisis; you must respect your hierarchy while maintaining a steady flow of information from top to bottom and bottom to top of your business.

The distinction between the roles and responsibilities of leaders and managers in effectively addressing and navigating through a crisis is referred to as the separation of leadership and management during a crisis. In this context, management is concerned with the operational components of the crisis. It entails managing the event's complexities, such as arranging resources, developing processes, and ensuring task execution runs well. Managers concentrate on the current facts and work tactically to resolve the crisis.

Leadership in a crisis, on the other hand, necessitates a broader view and an emphasis on change adaptation. Leaders take a step back from the details and take a broader strategic look at the situation. They examine the ramifications of the crisis, analyze it from multiple viewpoints, and make decisions that guide the organization through it. In a crisis, leadership frequently entails inspiring and motivating others, encouraging collaboration, and offering direction. They provide direction, instill confidence, and collaborate with stakeholders and decision-makers to make educated decisions.

To become a great leader, it is critical to spend quality time reflecting and developing networking skills. You are taking on the role of stage director, while your management team serves as the major performers on stage.

Instead of getting caught up in the details, concentrate on developing relationships with other stakeholders and decision-makers. Connecting with various groups is an important aspect of crisis leadership. As John C.

Maxwell reminds us: "Lots of people communicate but very few connect."[37] While modern technology helps in connecting the dots during a crisis, it is critical to prepare yourself and your team for the absence of such connections. A crisis initially focuses on your internal relationships with those closest to you, such as family, high-level executives, management, and ownership. After you have calmed down by assessing the state of your immediate social support, you must tap into the resources in your network. The more individuals who are connected to each other on numerous levels, the better off everyone will be.

Developing networking abilities is also essential for becoming a successful leader. Despite their widespread usage in addressing complex problems, the dissemination of time-sensitive information and the necessity for coordination provide significant obstacles for networks during catastrophic events. Extreme catastrophes are complex because of their uniqueness, which necessitates a continually evolving interaction across multiple organizations as the event evolves. As the crisis progresses, random networks emerge, which eventually give way to more ordered clusters. At the start of a disaster, create a communication tree with your organization to link the critical individuals, relay priorities, and use a funnel technique to ease communication.

As part of the first emergency team response (ETR) development, crisis leadership comprises building clusters and getting them to communicate efficiently in a dependable way for all participants.

To achieve immediate goals, keep the chain of command concise, with only the most relevant team leaders. Miscommunications or a lack of inter-departmental communication, as well as a lack of interrelationships amongst emergency services, have occasionally caused mayhem during emergencies, compounding the crisis.

While fire, police, and hospital institutions are key nodes in an emergency response network, the presence of cross over between these organizations enabling two-way information exchange is not always obvious. Even when people are only a few feet apart, network gaps can

---

37   John Maxell, "The Journey to Expert Communication: John Maxwell's 4 Stages of Communication Growth," Maxwell Leadership, April 4, 2023, https://www. maxwellleadership.com/blog/john-maxwells-4-stages-of-communication-growth/

prohibit the reciprocal flow of crucial information. Although Mayor Giuliani had good intentions when he issued a Mayoral Executive Order in 1997 designed to establish response protocols around a central command post to facilitate communications, the response to the World Trade Center incident highlighted the detrimental effects of a fragmented command structure comprised of organizational silos in the first hours of this tragic event. As emergency responders arrived on the scene, they built ad hoc networks and established distinct organizational commands in various areas, resulting in a fragmented emergency response that hampered information flow among incident commanders. "Operations during a crisis should be decentralized, but decision-making should not be."[38]

Similarly, Hurricane Katrina's network study revealed disconnects between city, state, and federal institutions, resulting in fragmented command structures, delays in resource distribution, and loss of life. Julie Reynolds in her report published in September of 2015 states:

The combination of unorganized and unmapped channels of communication at local, state, regional, and federal levels, and equipment damage from the storm resulted in this ultimate failure of communication. A method of fluid communication and information sharing and the ability to coordinate tasks, would have facilitated a more swift and functional reaction to the devastation.[39]

In a crisis, leaders must flatten the command hierarchy and eliminate work duplication by subordinates to enhance collaboration and coordination across all levels. In the early hours of a crisis, it is natural to want to find solutions for everyone at the same time, but everyone works together as one united front. Limit the hierarchy and assign one person to each function and duty within your agreed-upon ETR goals. Getting the right information at the right moment is critical.

---

38   Paul A. Argenti, "Crisis Communication: Lessons from 9/11," Harvard Business Review, December 2002, https://hbr.org/2002/12/crisis-communication-lessons-from-911.

39   Julie Reynolds, "Katrina Response: A Failure to Communicate," Veoci, September 2, 2015, https://veoci.com/blog/katrina-response-a-failure-to-communicate#:~:text=With%20landline%20telephones%2C%20radio%20antennas,3%20days%20following%20the%20hurricane.

Various teams, frameworks, and processes are established in response to a crisis, and their names should reflect what they do: Crisis Response Team, COVID-19 Task Force, Outbreak Management Team, War Room, Emergency Coordination Command Centre, Disaster Management Committee, or, in our case in Fort McMurray during the wildfires and flood, the Regional Emergency Operations Centre (REOC). Despite the different names, these groups usually have similar goals and are comprise of a central decision-making body. Those in charge have three main obligations: ensuring a constant and efficient flow of information across the ranks; optimizing the gathering, sharing, and distribution of critical information; and fostering coordination and collaboration among internal and external key stakeholders.

An efficient political decision-making framework in a crisis necessitates striking a delicate balance between conflicting interests. It must be small enough to make quick decisions but large enough to incorporate different perspectives and information sources. It must have a hierarchical structure with clear responsibilities, but it must also be flat and vertical to avoid suppressing criticism, groupthink, and centralizing decision-making power.

Finally, it must act decisively. Rivalries between internal or external groups' resources may impede progress during the initial recovery steps as everyone tries to understand the enormity of the damages or the true impact of a disaster. In Fort McMurray, the REOC was initially extraordinarily successful in limiting damages and loss of life, with only two casualties.

While constructive postmortems of a crisis are vital, undermining acts and decisions made during a crisis should be carefully evaluated and treated opportunistically rather than destructively. Our emotional and motivational states have a considerable influence on our decision-making powers, and our emotions can alter problem-solving efficacy and consequently the outcome of events, so it is critical to consider our emotional condition when making decisions during a crisis.

Leaders should make every effort to quickly align everyone by establishing clear standards and imposing strong timetables for relevant and up-to-date feedback. Although I had participated in a few pre-emptive preparedness sessions prior to the wildfires, the REOC established procedures to ensure a unified command process in the early hours of the Fort McMurray wildfires. They used numerous techniques to accomplish this. The command structure was developed by the REOC, which included representatives from numerous agencies and organizations participating in the response effort. This structure allowed for cooperation and collaboration among various parties.

Regular communication. The cooperating agencies created effective and consistent communication channels. This facilitated the exchange of information, updates, and directions, ensuring that everyone had the information they needed to make informed judgments.

Information sharing. The REOC established methods for all responding agencies to share information and situational awareness. This permitted a thorough grasp of the unfolding situation and coordinated reactions.

Joint planning. The REOC conducted joint planning sessions in which representatives from several agencies worked together to create a single response plan. This guaranteed that all responding entities' activities and objectives were consistent. The REOC used incident action planning, which entailed creating a coherent strategy outlining the objectives, strategies, and tactics for managing the wildfires. This plan supervised all responding agencies' actions and guaranteed a coordinated approach.

Integrated operations. The REOC promoted integrated operations by bringing together resources from many agencies to work seamlessly together. This approach enabled better resource allocation, effort coordination, and response capability optimization.

I strongly advise any municipality or comparable institution to follow the procedures outlined above to develop a solid framework for dealing with any form of emergency disaster. To this day, these crucial procedures have preserved most of the town from the Beast and its residents, including myself, teams, and families.

Collaborate

Extreme occurrences, such as terrorism, natural disasters, or major catastrophes, swiftly overwhelm department heads, leaders, and the primary agency in charge of the emergency response. It is clear from the start of the crisis that other agencies and organizations, as well as their individual leaders, will be requested to assist. Events unfold rapidly, putting everyone under pressure to work together. Other agencies and public services will need to adjust quickly and develop a communication system that allows them to fully interact and leverage each other's strengths and capacities.

The attitude of collaboration between my properties was critical to our team's survival and the speedy establishment of internal communications. Other residences in Alberta promptly offered to help welcome evacuees and their families.

In hospitals, it is normal for surgical team members to identify themselves at the start of surgery. This gesture gives nurses the same standing as surgeons in terms of speaking out when something does not appear to be right. Similarly, as new participants from multiple agencies emerge in emergency meetings and group conversations, members of a unified command team must introduce themselves and exchange ideas throughout the crisis. Decision-makers should go around to each agency delegate at the opening of the first interagency meeting, shake hands, and identify themselves by name and role.

As a result, information sharing, and collaboration will improve. People will feel more at ease discussing comments and concerns if they feel like they are part of a team.

A flattened command necessitates the development of good negotiating abilities for complex multi-party involvement during extreme situations by crisis leaders. Mutual decision-making requires leaders to be accountable not just for the activities of their respective groups but also for all incident outcomes. Leaders must learn to exchange information, listen to others' concerns, articulate essential issues, and collaborate to create a consensus on incident management objectives and common goals.

Coordination

Coordination is of paramount importance during times of crisis caused by natural disasters. The seamless collaboration and organization among various entities, including government agencies, emergency responders, relief organizations, and the affected community, can significantly impact the effectiveness of response and recovery efforts.

Without proper coordination, multiple agencies or groups might inadvertently work on the same tasks, leading to inefficiencies, wasted resources, and confusion. Coordination ensures that efforts are complementary rather than duplicative.

Coordination also facilitates the sharing of real-time information and updates about the disaster's evolving situation. This information helps decision-makers adjust strategies and resources as needed.

Natural disasters often leave behind long-lasting impacts. Coordinated recovery efforts help communities rebuild infrastructure, restore essential services, and provide psychological support to survivors.

During the wildfires and floods, coordination among our personnel was critical. We had the appropriate individuals in the proper roles, and we had a great deal of respect and trust for one another. Prior to these events, our front office, cleaning, maintenance, and, of course, hotel general managers all worked in separate silos. They were, nevertheless, responsible for completing numerous initiatives in which collaboration across all departments of all eight of our properties was part of our day-to-day operations. This mental attitude encouraged everyone to work together and made it a lot simpler for everyone when we had to pull together under tremendous duress to plan everyone's safety and evacuation.

A culture of mutual respect, accountability, and trust supports successful coordination. It promotes open communication, collaboration, teamwork, individual accountability, adaptation, and flexibility. Organizations that cultivate such a culture have a better chance of emerging stronger and more resilient after a disaster.

"THEM," Being Resilient

The community of Fort McMurray had already been severely impacted by the abrupt drop in the price of a barrel of oil, which began in 2014 and had a terrible effect on the local economy. This, combined with the May 2016 wildfires, continued economic downturn, the extraordinary April 2020 floods, and the COVID-19 epidemic, has resulted in Fort McMurray being resilient. Throughout these events, I regularly heard the word "resilience" invoked.

So, what exactly is resilience? According to the American Psychological Association, "Resilience is the process and outcome of successfully adapting to difficult or challenging life experiences, especially through mental, emotional, and behavioral flexibility and adjustment to external and internal demands."[40]

Managing a crisis can be extremely taxing on a leader's mental health. As a result, taking some "me time" is critical, even if certain stakeholders and the media disagree. During the Ottawa bridge blockage caused by the Freedom Convoy, for example, Ontario Premier Doug Ford was chastised by a journalist for taking some personal time and going skiing for a few hours. Premier Ford defended his behaviour, reminding the journalist that he routinely accepts calls until midnight and begins at 6:00 a.m. This was a wise decision since leaders may strategize inwardly and replenish their adrenaline, which helps to balance their amygdala.

It is critical for a leader to manage the media carefully during a crisis. I learned the value of being prepared when working with the media during the Fort McMurray disasters in 2016 and 2020. I established a list of vital

---

40   "Resilience," American Psychology Association, accessed November 13, 2023, https:// www.apa.org/topics/resilience.

information I wanted to transmit and ensured that I managed their queries efficiently in the initial hours of each crisis. Although it is critical to realize the opportunity that interviews might give, it is also critical to be prepared and to decline interviews when other operational activities require your entire focus.

We must realize the impact that uncertainty has on the people who drive the company. During such moments, emotional intelligence is essential. Resilient leaders show empathy and compassion for the human cost of disruption, understanding that their staff members' attention has shifted from their regular work responsibilities to concerns about the health of their immediate family, the closure of schools, and the unpredictable nature of current events endangering their own livelihood and well-being.

These leaders also instill in their team members a calm and deliberate approach, encouraging them to face whatever problems lie ahead. Even a few minutes spent together might provide a sense of alignment and brief clarity during these stressful times.

A Few Principles in Resilience

Tenacity is a critical component of resilience because it determines how people react to failure. It gives them the confidence to tackle obstacles head on, learn from their mistakes, and keep moving forward with resolve. The relationship between tenacity and failure in resilience emphasizes the significance of maintaining a positive and persistent perspective in the face of life's unavoidable failures.

Leaders can intentionally practice and conduct the discipline of overcoming obstacles, problems, and failures in life and at work.

While the specific parts may change based on the circumstances and severity of the crisis, here are some core resilience principles for you and your organization to follow:

Preparedness. The foundation of resilience is initiative-taking planning and preparedness. You can never be sufficiently prepared for a crisis. You are prepared to fail by failing to prepare. Identifying potential risks, understanding their consequences, and adopting strategies and resources to minimize and respond to those risks are all part of this process.

Establishing communication channels, protocols, and coordination structures to enable rapid and effective response during a crisis is also part of preparedness. This is a collaborative effort! Witnessing so many catastrophes, I urge that all businesses, cities, and various governmental entities create an emergency plan.

Flexibility and adaptability. The ability to adapt to changing conditions is required for resilience. Individuals, communities, organizations, and systems that are adaptable can change their tactics, operations, and plans in reaction to unforeseen circumstances. Accepting innovation, learning from prior experiences, and being open to new ways are critical for effectively responding during a crisis.

Redundancy and robustness. Resilient systems have redundancy and robustness built in to resist shocks and disturbances. This can include essential infrastructure redundancy, backup systems, diverse supply chains, and numerous communication channels. Having backup options and alternative channels can lessen the impact of failures or disruptions and facilitate recovery.

Resilience is built on resourcefulness. Make the most of available resources and produce inventive solutions to problems. This could include repurposing existing assets, engaging with other stakeholders, and mobilizing community networks and social capital. When faced with limited resources during a crisis, resourcefulness allows for more efficient and effective actions. Do not be scared to seek out hidden skills within your team! You do not know everything!

Developing resilience in leaders begins with the formation and cultivation of networks. When confronted with stressful or overwhelming events, confiding in trusted friends and coworkers can help lessen the load. These peers can offer advice and support, which is especially crucial for leaders who want to stay resilient. Having a varied network of people with different skills and viewpoints can also help move significant projects forward.

Communication and information sharing. When there are strong channels of communication both inside and between organizations and communities, resilience is improved. Sharing information, issuing alerts, coordinating actions, and helping can improve collective understanding, cooperation, and decision-making, allowing for a more organized and successful response.

Community engagement. Resilience is about the collective strength of communities, not just individual or organizational capacities. Effective crisis management requires the development of social cohesion, trust, and community engagement. Strong social networks, mutual support, and open decision-making procedures promote resilience by encouraging collaboration, cooperation, and a sense of belonging. Recognizing and celebrating little accomplishments can assist leaders in cultivating a more positive mindset. Leaders can build an overall happy culture by practising gratitude for the minor things that provide delight in the workplace. Small victories increase team spirit. Leaders should not wait for big wins to laud their teams. Instead, frequent acknowledgment motivates and inspires the workforce. When a leader recognizes modest victories, especially during challenging times, trust is developed.

Continuity and recovery. Resilience entails planning for continuity and recovery even during a crisis. This includes both short-term response measures and long-term recovery activities. Resilience requires the development of techniques and processes to restore key services, repair devastated places, help affected people, and improve psychological well-being.

Learning and adaptation. Resilience is a constant process of learning from one's experiences and adjusting to new obstacles. It includes performing postcrisis evaluations and debriefings, as well as identifying and incorporating lessons learned into future planning and preparedness activities. Embracing a culture of learning and adaptation contributes to the development of a more resilient society over time.

Resilience in Financing

Resilient leaders must maintain financial stability not only for the sake of their employees, customers, and investors but also to defend their organization's financial performance. Making hard, fact-based judgments while focusing on cash flow is important.

In the early hours of fleeing the inferno, my immediate thoughts were about which and how many assets (hotel properties) the company may lose, wreaking havoc on our employees with serious societal ramifications. I was able to keep the morale up as thankfully, the owners and the management company maintained regular payrolls for all of us despite receiving no revenues as our properties were all closed for a lengthy period.

However, numerous others did not profit from such kindness, and terrible hardship befell individuals and businesses, with many of them never returning to work or live in Fort McMurray. During a crisis or a great existential catastrophe, the adage "cash is king" is true. I am not an accountant, but I would humbly offer the following financial guidelines to follow during and after the crisis:

Create and sustain a crisis command centre. As mentioned in this book, you should have a rallying centre where significant and timely financial decisions can be made. Because there are numerous mini-crises to manage in addition to the major one, decentralizing decision-making may be required for consistency, speed, and, most importantly, decisiveness, as uncertainty might paralyze certain decision-makers. But make sure you create ground rules for everyone involved. By bringing key decision-makers and specialists together, the organization will have access to crucial and immediate information, expertise, and resources, enabling quick responses while absorbing immediate and possible financial costs and risks.

Assess talent and strategy support. We all know "It's lonely at the top!" but use personnel you have complete trust in to manage certain duties that have significant monetary impact.

Assess critical responsibilities and skills. Identify the critical responsibilities and skills needed to keep essential operations running and the crisis response strategy in place. I made the most of my team leaders' knowledge by matching our needs with their talents as we worked through these difficulties. Determine which positions are crucial to business continuity and prioritize your assistance to them.

Conduct a skills gap analysis. Compare the existing workforce's abilities and competencies to the important jobs and skills specified. Determine any gaps that could impede effective crisis management and resilience.

Maintain business continuity and funding. In our situation, during the start of the wildfires, business at our hotels vanished in a matter of hours. Make sure to outline the brutal truth about your financial status as it unfolds throughout the course of the crisis to all parties involved. Maintain open and transparent communication with lenders and investors to assure their continued support. Keep them up to date on the company's financial condition, prospective crisis implications, and mitigation efforts. If necessary, investigate supplementary financing or a credit line.

Investigate cost-cutting measures without jeopardizing vital functions. If you work in the service sector, as we did, make sure your front line has all the tools and assistance they need to establish excellent guest interactions. Contracts should be renegotiated, inventory should be optimized, and personnel alterations should be considered. This is the most difficult assignment for you to complete because it is likely that some of your faithful employees will not return into your fold. If you must lay off staff, do so face-to-face. This is not the time to hide behind your computer!

Investigate government assistance programs. Stay informed or have someone inform you about what loans, programs, and grants are available. Throughout the crisis, we reached out to municipal, provincial, and federal officials. Some recovery support mechanisms worked well for us, while others did not. However, create or convene a task committee to examine and evaluate eligibility requirements.

Supplies. Some of your usual supplies and suppliers may be disrupted. Maintain current and strong relationships with your suppliers while maintaining frequent communication with them and responding quickly to any issues or disruptions. At the start of COVID-19, we, like everyone else, were challenged with PPE supplies. I made certain that we had a centralized system in place to efficiently supply all our properties with stringent, daily inventory management and delivery. You must exercise caution since some managers may hoard resources to the detriment of others.

Improve digital capabilities. This is an area that we all learned rapidly, particularly in the domain of communication with the help of Zoom, Teams, Webex, and similar mediums. Again, capitalizing on the talent we had on board, I was fortunate to have Mike Harlick as my second-in-command who thankfully is a virtuoso in these innovative technologies when the rest of us are not. With the dangers of germs and the uncertainty around COVID-19, I made digitization procedures and services a top priority. We identified important processes and services that may be digitized to reduce physical contact and allow remote operations. Digital document management, inventory management, online payment systems, virtual customer care, and e-commerce platforms are all examples of this. Digital process simplification improves efficiency and robustness.

However, even during a crisis, a company's purpose should remain unwavering, as it is never negotiable. Purpose is the location of the head and heart units. Although many firms today have established a mission other than profit, it runs the risk of being overlooked in day-to-day choices. According to a 2016 survey, "79 percent of business executives agree that an organization's mission is critical to its success, yet 68 percent shared that purpose is not used as a guidepost in leadership decision making processes within their organization."[41]

We frequently see organizations in crisis that are dealing with a slew of pressing difficulties on multiple fronts. Resilient leaders prioritize the most critical issues and generate focal points that spread swiftly throughout the organization.

Personal Log: Fort McMurray, Alberta, May to June 2016 and May 2020: Through Hell and High Water!

During these two major crises, I had to deal with the media and their relentless pursuit of information about my experiences. Within hours of both crises, radio stations were calling me for interviews to get my perspective on the events unfolding. To ensure that I conveyed the information I deemed pertinent, I created a brief list on my phone and used their questions as a guide for my responses. It is essential to be prepared and conduct some research before answering any calls or radio interviews. If you have pressing tasks at hand, however, decline politely and schedule another time for the interview.

When the disastrous flood occurred, the media once again sought immediate feedback. In the early hours of the flood, my phone rang

---

41 Caterina Bulgarella, "Purpose-Driven Companies Evolve Faster Than Others," Forbes, September 21, 2018, https://www.forbes.com/sites/caterinabulgarella/2018/09/21/purpose-driven-companies-evolve-faster-than-others/?sh=335efc5f55bc.

incessantly, but I could not provide updates as I did not have access to our properties and the entire downtown area was sealed by police.

I caution individuals who want to help by informing the public of a particular situation when it is unclear. There is a tendency to communicate assertively that the "situation is under control" when several obstacles and challenges lie ahead. It is best to relay personal situations and state only known facts, promising the media further information with no definite deadline when available.

The surface destruction caused by the floods was as bad as the destruction beneath the surface. Flooded foundations, sewer lines, gas lines, and other infrastructure resulted in dire consequences for citizens living downtown. Many of them lost their dwellings twice in a row, some of which they had just rebuilt after the wildfires.

The Leader in Public

Senior executives are frequently hesitant to meet with the media, especially when under duress. Unless you have prior experience managing such situations, I recommend entrusting them to your public relations firm; however, as a public figure, you should demonstrate strength and control, which can help both internal and external stakeholders.

During a crisis, there is a tug of war between avoiding media duties and demonstrating command and compassion for those affected. Both social media and traditional media battle for your attention and statements, adding tension to an already stressful situation. If you have time to prepare, I recommend that you do the following:

Make a list of what you should and should not say. Because the interviewer may attempt to divert the topic, you must stay focused on your point.

Prepare meaningful and concise key messages. Avoid talking about topics with which you are unfamiliar. You should target the most critical issues and create focal points that can quickly spread throughout the organization. Prioritize to the media the area of focus of those who are most important to you, such as your employees and direct stockholders.

Be mindful of how you speak. Address the media in a controlled, firm voice while reaffirming the positive and optimistic measures accomplished thus far. Avoid speaking about the future because uncontrollable circumstances can come back to harm you. Authenticity is essential; if you lack understanding on a certain issue, confess it and return to the topic later if necessary. Speak in short and measured phrases, with restraint, and with a gap between phrases. Injecting some levity into demanding situations can also help relieve tension. During his bunker press appearances, for example, Ukrainian President Zelenskyy, under tense pressure, showed his talents for spontaneity, irony, and sarcasm. While it is not necessary to deliver jokes, having a sense of humour might help one maintain their sanity during tough times.

During interviews, the media may try to trap you with dramatic circumstances to get attention and market share. To counteract this, recall the primary messaging tone you established to oversee the problem. Expect little pity or appreciation from the media since they are simply doing their job and will quickly move on to the next story.

When dealing with criticism, keep in mind that loud detractors are sometimes unaware of the leader's actions. While it is critical not to ignore the noise, it is even more necessary to reassure relevant stakeholders.

Managing social media during a crisis can be difficult, so I suggest forming a task force to monitor and respond to various postings, comments, and updates.

Optimism should be encouraged while confronting the brutal facts to avoid future misunderstandings or interpretations of actions or inactions. Leaders may demonstrate strength and compassion while reducing stress by handling media relations appropriately.

Personal Reflections on "THEM"

As the crisis unfolds with multiple layers of complexities and challenges, you will soon find out that external support and resources will become your own lifeline. But I stress the importance of initially mastering the two previous disciplines of managing yourself and your immediate leadership team.

Bringing external resources to a disjointed or leaderless organization will make the situation even worse, to the point where it could cost lives and consequentially damage structural assets.

In the first few hours of your own crisis, you will get an unimaginable number of calls from people you have barely heard of offering their support and good thoughts. Although this is comforting, your immediate priorities are your own survival and trying to make sense of the surrounding madness. But after a few hours and days of successfully attempting to control the events as much as you can, you will have to call on external resources for you and your team to gain the upper hand.

External resources would provide additional expertise, workforce, skills, and infrastructure, allowing you a more comprehensive response. Do not be shy about asking the experts if some of them are around you or can be reached. You do not know it all! External resources bring fresh perspectives and alternative viewpoints that can lead you to innovative ways to address your issues, concerns, and dilemmas. As you surround yourself with the best, take the same approach to getting the help you need for a particular task you may not be comfortable dealing with.

Lots of people want to help you, but make sure you know the specific gaps where you need help and by whom. Be sensitive to people who are willing to help but may sound like they are using your time and patience when, in turn, they are all trying to support you and your team. I mentioned how your local partnerships and networking have a tremendous role to play. These will be extraordinarily helpful in leveraging support and collaboration. But everyone has their own limits and budgets, and if your requests may be too much of an "ask," be thankful in any case because you may get the support you need a few hours or days later! You never know when the same person may come back to you and get you the help you need. It happened to me on many occasions when I requested some resources that were initially denied but later provided with ample results.

Your pool of known stakeholders needs to be engaged, which has multiple effects on fostering coordination and collaboration among all concerned, but again, these need to be managed carefully.

Time is a unique external and often invaluable resource in times of crisis. Because you are bombarded with an immense number of tasks and follow-ups while handling your own state of mind and continuing to motivate your team, you will quickly find that time is a rare commodity. Using time wisely and allocating specific times for you to practice your internal over your external communications, coordination, and collaboration will be essential. This will help you overcome the need to be available to everyone all the time and find balance.

PART FOUR:
ME, US, AND THEM AND
THE NEXT CRISIS

"ME," "US," and "THEM"
Standing Down the Crisis

The last act of a play serves to reveal, resolve, or explain, the questions, conflicts, and relationships introduced in the play's content. There are some scenes and dialogue that may linger in your mind for a few days before being forgotten. A crisis has a similar effect in that subsequent events or crises may be pushed out of the spotlight; however, the aftermath of a crisis can have a dramatic and long-lasting impact on an individual's worldview.

The impacts of a crisis are not restricted to the weeks immediately following the event. Rather, a crisis can cause a form of PTSD that differs from person to person for months, if not years, afterwards. It is natural to experience a sense of control, victory, and pride when a crisis has passed, but it is critical not to let one's ego take over. Reflect, do postmortems, and evaluate what changes and practices are required to be better prepared for the next crisis, not only for yourself but also for the team and the company.

Personal Log: Fort McMurray, Alberta, June 17, 2016, 5:30 p.m.: Through Hell!

After two weeks of arranging our team leaders, staff, and families into various properties in Alberta, it was time to regroup and start the process of re-entry into the city. We needed to become the beachhead in getting our properties back to operational status and allow the skeleton crew to get basic services back up and running; however, as most of us did not have a clear idea of what we would find ex; the amount of disinfection, cleaning, and repairs needed to get our services up and running.

It was time to shake up the team. The majority of them had been idle and in limbo on when and if they would return. Luckily, they were benefiting from ongoing wages paid thanks to the generosity of the ownership of Morguard and the management company at Atlific. I asked volunteers to come back with me, but it was difficult to convince them as they were extremely concerned about their health and the effects for their young families. To keep morale up, we organized outings to local locations, and created some team activities.

One morning, I summoned the troops and asked for their continuous commitment not only to our organization but also to the city, which needed us to start the rebuilding process. I was direct and blunt, telling the brutal facts. Now was the time to give back as a sign of gratitude to everyone who had helped us during these last dramatic weeks. I did not receive a rousing standing ovation, but a steady flow of concerns about their safety and that of their families. I then had no choice but to be more assertive and ask for an initial small contingent of team members who were single or wouldn't be severely impacted by having their families return, to go up first and get a sense of the realities in town.

We would later prepare for a larger group to come once we had an initial grasp of the challenges ahead, allowing for a disciplined re-entry for the rest of our members.

The first report from these courageous team members confirmed that all our properties were still standing, but there were lots of damages in various parts of the city.

My wife, our faithful dog Jaxx, and I, arrived in a deserted town that had an eerie feeling of the "morning after" type of disaster movie following a nuclear war or apocalypse. There were no sounds; no one on the streets, but a few police cars who maintained strategic entrance points. This was a unique feeling, but we had to overcome this sense of loss, as the challenge ahead was enormous to get back to a relative sense of business as usual.

Timing Is Everything

The importance of timing cannot be overstated. Countless people have made premature calls to end the crisis. Everyone remembers President Bush's statement on the deck of an aircraft carrier with the "Mission Accomplished" banner in the background only for the war to continue years after. I recall seeing Chief Darby Allen, in command of our Fort McMurray fire department, declare the situation under control, with things spinning out of control just hours later.

I sympathize with leaders who want to restore normalcy as soon as possible. Going through a crisis is incredibly taxing, and the consequences can be severe. The desire to return to normalcy is reasonable, as evidenced by the on-and-off COVID limitations, where multiple changes of direction produced confusion.

Standing down or demobilizing the crisis team leadership, to borrow a military word, is a complex undertaking. I want to underline that this is the time for leaders to demonstrate empathy. Moving from a high-adrenaline state to a sense of normalcy might result in emotional situations, such as alienation, desertion, or a lack of purpose. If professional counsellors are available, make sure that all team members are aware of how to receive help and that this service is offered throughout the organization, emphasizing privacy and anonymity.

Dam the paperwork! ... Not in this case. As soon as you and your team regain a sense of normalcy, instruct all teams and committees to collect data, reports, and other documents that could help another team experiencing similar circumstances; you never know as you and your team, family, and friends could be thrown in a comparable situation. It happened to us! While this procedure may be time-consuming, it is required since insurance companies and lawyers may demand data and information to assist with a case or claim on behalf of the firm or a member of your team.

It's me time! Take some time for personal thought while the situation is still fresh in your mind. You will not have all the answers or recommendations, but you are looking for personal closure rather than tackling all the world's problems.

Rally the troops. After your teams have had some "me time," get them back into the rhythm that existed before the events. A crisis can have devastating material and psychological consequences, leaving individuals and organizations heartbroken and depleted of vitality.

This is a good opportunity to question the status quo and strive to do better next time. A crisis is frequently a catalyst for fresh chances.

Leadership in the post-crisis era is all about timing and balance. Speaking about renewal too soon cannot address the bodily and mental anguish, while failing to move towards renewal risks being imprisoned in survival mode. I often warn about getting into a habit and being naive to the threat of oncoming disaster because crises may creep up on any firm or organization. According to the Federal Emergency Management Agency, "40% of businesses do not reopen following a disaster. On top of that, another 20% fail within one year."[42]

Small business operators disregard the environment as a significant component affecting their company's crisis readiness. In the survey report *A Crisis of Confidence* by Deloitte Touche Tohmatsu Limited, it states:

> Board members around the world have confidence in their organizations' ability to deal with crisis situations (76%), but they are less confident that they—and their organizations—are prepared for a crisis . . .. Fewer than half (49%) of 317 board members surveyed say their organizations have the capabilities or processes in place required to manage a crisis with the best possible outcome.[43]

I strongly encourage businesses to be prepared for any catastrophe, and I hope that this book can educate executives on how to prepare for and manage a crisis. Ignoring such incidents could have devastating effects for their organizations, resulting in human and physical losses.

---

42 "Study: 40% of Businesses Fail to Reopen after a Disaster," Access, last modified April 14, 2020, https://www.accesscorp.com/en-ca/press-coverage/ study-40-percent-businesses-fail-reopen-disaster/.

43 "Gaps Exist in Board Members' Crisis Awareness, Preparedness: Global Survey," The Wall Street Journal, accessed November 13, 2023, https://deloitte.wsj.com/ riskandcompliance/gaps-exist-in-board-members-crisis-awareness- preparedness-global-survey-01671228529.

"ME," "US," and "THEM"
and Steps to Prepare for the Next Crisis

The post-climatic period following the wildfires and floods has had a lasting impact on all citizens who experienced these dramatic events. Reflecting on my individual experiences, I have witnessed the profound impact of various catastrophic events, such as the wildfires in 2016, the flooding in 2020, and the ongoing challenges posed by the COVID-19 pandemic. It is evident that these instances have left a lasting mark, not only on the physical landscape but also on the mental well-being of the affected communities.

Studies conducted in the aftermath of these events have shed light on the prevalence of PTSD-like symptoms among residents.[44] These investigations have delved into sociological and clinical risk factors, revealing a complex interplay between external circumstances and mental health outcomes. The goal has been to gain a deeper understanding of the recovery process and its implications for mental health, aiming to better tailor support for those who are particularly vulnerable to the aftermath of such natural disasters.

It is worth noting that the challenges presented by the COVID-19 pandemic have introduced a unique set of obstacles. The necessity of physical separation and stringent sanitation measures has added layers of complexity to evacuation procedures, post-disaster regulations, and the

---

44 Genevieve Belleville, Marie-Christine Ouellet, and Charles M. Morin, "Post-Traumatic Stress among Evacuees from the 2016 Fort McMurray Wildfires: Exploration of Psychological and Sleep Symptoms Three Months after the Evacuation," International Journal of Environmental Research and Public Health 16, no. 9 (May 8, 2019): 1604, doi: 10.3390/ijerph16091604.

overall recovery process. This, in turn, has compounded the physical and economic toll of traumatic experiences, casting a shadow on survivors' emotional well-being.

My own observations underscore the intricate web that ties together physical and emotional dimensions in the face of adversity. As we navigate through these challenges, it becomes increasingly vital to cultivate a comprehensive approach that addresses both the immediate and long-term well-being of those affected. Through collective effort and a deepened understanding of the nuances at play, we can strive to restore not only the physical environments but also the emotional resilience of our communities.

Having gone through these natural disaster crises, many residents, and many people in Fort McMurray experienced symptoms of PTSD. The experience of losing homes, possessions, and communities, as well as the ongoing stress and uncertainty of the events, had and continues to have a significant impact on mental health. Many residents also reported feeling overwhelmed by the media's attention and the constant need to update friends and family on their safety and well-being, which added to the stress and trauma of the events.

My ears perk up every spring and summer when I hear helicopters dispatched from the forestry government agencies. This sound has some visceral meaning to my subconscious, which I will keep stored in the deepest part of my brain, hoping my amygdala will not once again be put on active alert mode caused by another dramatic event.

There are three steps you can take to prepare yourself, team, and internal and external stakeholders:

Step one: reality check

Humanity has evolved over generations with its natural sense of optimism. Leaders have a natural feeling of optimism that often borders on arrogance. This might lead to a false sense of invincibility, making individuals more vulnerable overall. Having been a part of many local business strategies, planning sessions, and budget conversations throughout my career, I can count on one hand the number of times we have explored what-if scenarios in any significant sense during an annual business plan.

What can happen to a firm during a crisis is left to the imagination of its executives, and those responsible for charting the road forward may limit a company's resilience during a crisis. Leaders must return to basics and focus on addressing the following five W's:

- What do we know so far?

- When did it happen?

- Where did it take place?

- Who has been impacted?

- Why do we need to take specific actions?

Leaders can respond to crises more successfully if they have a framework in place that allows them to address these key issues.

Step two: create a crisis-ready culture

Creating a crisis-ready culture begins with instilling a high degree of trust throughout the business, resulting in a profound sense of openness at all levels. Mistakes are controllable, and vulnerability serves as a catalyst for course adjustments along the way. A crisis will merely reaffirm what the organization should accomplish daily, only exacerbated by the exigencies of the situation. There is a significant difference between a leader's aim and their deeds. Confronting the harsh facts and knowing where your organization is and where it wants to go will help you prepare for oncoming catastrophes.

Create a detailed crisis-management plan. Create a strategy that explains the duties and responsibilities of everyone in the organization during a crisis. The plan should also include a communication strategy, incident response procedures, and business continuity standards.

Employees should receive crisis-management training. Hold frequent training sessions to educate personnel on how to respond to various crises. This involves equipping them with the tools and resources they need to effectively manage crises.

The "trust" factor. Encourage employees to speak out about potential dangers and issues that could lead to a disaster by cultivating a "trust culture." This necessitates the creation of an environment in which employees feel safe reporting problems without fear of retaliation.

Run regular crisis scenarios. Simulations allow staff to practice their crisis-management abilities in a safe environment. This allows the company to identify and address holes in its crisis-management plan. Regularly review and update this plan. A crisis management strategy should be a live document that is reviewed and updated on a regular basis. This guarantees that it remains relevant and effective in reacting to new and emerging threats.

Lead by example. Leaders should set the tone for the organization by demonstrating their commitment to crisis management. This includes being open and honest, speaking clearly and effectively, and accepting responsibility when things go wrong.

Step three: be strategic

Three levels of your ERT are necessary, with specific responsibilities around strategic, operational, and functional needs.

Strategic needs. This is usually the top level of your leadership team. Their focus is on critical decisions to make, good or bad! Mid- to long-term affects strategies, commercial, and organizational immediacy, and recovery. Most of these would be conducted under the "ME" approach!

Operational needs. At the "US" level, reliable and robust communication systems are crucial for coordination among team members. This includes radios, satellite phones, and other means of communication. Establish a command centre with the necessary technology and infrastructure to manage and coordinate the emergency response.

Functional needs. At the "THEM" level, focus on external communications, legal, human resources, financial needs, cash flow management, regulatory compliance, government relations, security, and IT. These are just a few of the components and resources that make up functional demands.

This model may not be the most practical for your specific organization and may be too simplistic, but I caution the leader not to make their ERT too cumbersome with too many layers. Surviving a crisis is not a badge of honour, but a confirmation that your organization had a specific plan to survive it. Effective crisis leadership does not begin once a crisis happens, but well before the dramatic event.

"ME," "US," and "THEM"

Handling Losses

Are you like me, working hard every day and feeling stressed? Dealing with a significant crisis was not in your plans, and it may have shattered your hopes and objectives. When things return to normalcy, you may feel disoriented and unclear about what to do next; however, you cannot effectively lead beyond this catastrophe tomorrow if you do not take the time to mourn your loss of vision now. Here is how:

Set aside some time to reflect. Take the time to process what you have lost, both personally and professionally. Schedule time to digest your feelings and think about what you have gone through.

Write down your thoughts. After you have processed your feelings, write about what you have lost and how you feel. This will help you organize your thoughts and create clarity for your future steps. Make mental checklists of noteworthy events and conversations. Consider it another way: life has changed since the crisis, and it is difficult to adjust to the new normal yet change also brings new chances. Write down these opportunities and allow them to motivate you to forge a new route forward with hope. It is tough to be optimistic during a crisis. Negative replies and comments will exacerbate the situation. The best leaders take the time to contemplate, mourn, and embrace loss. They used it to construct something greater, and they feel that the future may be brighter than the past.

Do your best with the best. You will produce your best work when surrounded by your best individuals. As I have stated, controlling a crisis begins with you! As you assessed the initial level of crisis, you would have built within your business a tight knit of top leaders who, given the opportunity to be analytical people, would have been ready to answer the call, reinforcing the deep level of trust you entrenched within the team.

Get your own "triple A" batteries—and more acronyms. (I am fond of them as you may have guessed!)

Assess the immediate circumstances it presented you with. This is a team effort! You are in crisis mode and have no time for egos or time wasted for lack of confronting the brutal realities. Time to lead, follow, or get out of the way!

Adapt, plan, and execute! Begin with the end goal in mind! Decide and allocate duties and responsibilities, and convey clarity and "elevator feedback," ensuring that information is cascading up and down, down, and up through the ranks.

Accountability. Create defined protocols that allow everyone to sing from the same sheet of music. Break down the duties and timelines! Establish precise protocols that allow everyone to collaborate effortlessly toward the same goal.

Agility. This is your "spare battery." President John F. Kennedy demonstrated agility during the Cuban Missile Crisis in 1962 by widening his alternatives rather than mindlessly following one course of action.

Leaders can learn from past and present leaders who have led amid wars, crises, and political upheavals. Leaders should research historical leadership in their list of to-read books. Losses are seldom easy to accept. The more you and your team can prepare for dealing with loss, the simpler it will be to come out on the other side.

The Crisis as Seen from the Outside

Communication, or the lack thereof, can worsen the "ME and THEM" conundrum. Dealing with external parties, such as stakeholders, external resources, specialists, legal counsel, and insurance, requires meticulous planning prior to the crisis manifesting. This should be part of a communication plan that develops suitable communication tactics with the outside from the start. This plan should be adaptable, well-practised, and include facts necessary for sound decision-making. Processes should emphasize reaction mechanisms that are swift, accurate, and consistent.

Currently, an institution can either create or lose its reputation through a crisis, which can be orchestrated through social media and the media. Social media may spread information about a disaster quicker than an organization might think. Its content is inflammatory and incorporates rumourmongering, which could have a considerable impact on the leaders in charge of a crisis. However, if effectively managed, social media provides a plethora of chances for companies to manage their own crises. In our situation, it was a critical tool for communicating with our team leaders and members when local radios were down during the wildfires. During a crisis, the public and stakeholders want immediate information.

When confronted with external upheaval and tragedy, one seeks inner power to not only endure and appraise but also to overcome. Rather than focusing on what you can receive, consider the cards you have been dealt and what you can give back to your stakeholders. When we serve others, even in modest ways, our fear fades and our concentration sharpen.

Emphasize to your followers that you expect everyone, individually and as a group, to learn their way ahead, to experiment with new ways of working, to expect the occasional failure, and to rapidly pivot to a new task and figure out the future together.

The raison d'être is obvious in organizations that provide important services, such as government agencies, hospitals, pharmacies, grocery stores, food and healthcare equipment, manufacturing plants, news sources, research labs, and nonprofits that serve the disadvantaged.

It is nevertheless critical to underline the vital role that everyone involved in the operation performs. In other businesses, the new objective may be as basic as assisting all stakeholders in navigating the crisis as successfully as possible.

Navigating during a Crisis

Navigating and managing a crisis are two interwoven processes that involve diverse aspects of dealing with demanding situations. While navigating a crisis refers to finding a path or direction through the crisis, managing a crisis means actively managing and responding to the obstacles it poses.

Navigating a crisis emphasizes finding a route ahead amid uncertainty and turbulence. It entails assessing the issue, comprehending the scale and implications of the crisis, and identifying potential solutions or measures to manage it. This necessitates a larger viewpoint and the ability to examine the issue from different perspectives, considering numerous causes, parties, potential consequences. It includes establishing a plan, setting goals, and making strategic decisions to steer the crisis response.

This stage also includes the strategic and analytical process of charting a course through tough conditions, whereas crisis management entails the practical implementation of plans and activities to lessen the crisis's impact. Both components are critical for effectively managing a crisis and require a diverse set of abilities, including problem-solving, decision-making, adaptation, and leadership. A crisis is rarely a solitary trip. To deal with obstacles, it is common to rely on both formal and informal support structures. During challenging times, I have stressed the need for community resilience and solidarity—how people band together, support one another, and create a sense of belonging and hope in the middle of a catastrophe. To address the resulting confusion, clear communication is required.

Leaders must tell the truth clearly and prevent superfluous conversations or learning aloud. People rely on clarity, and even if there are no answers, plain and helpful truths are valued. Though it is difficult when there is so much unknown, mindfulness can assist. In times of crisis, you must control your own energy and emotions, as well as those of your team. Crises are tiring and can lead to burnout, especially for those who have lost loved ones.

Leaders must keep their fingers on the pulse of their people's energy and emotions and respond appropriately. They must understand when it is necessary to focus on work and when it is necessary to take a break for personal care. This includes taking care of their physical and emotional health, spending time outside, connecting with loved ones, and being device-free.

Leaders must demonstrate empathy and address everyone's anxieties and concerns while navigating the sea of unknowns and transparencies. Model the behaviour you want to see in others and utilize body language, words, and actions to show that you are pushing forward with conviction and courage. Check on the team's energy and emotions on a frequent basis and encourage rest and recharge. Encourage gratitude by asking team members to write down three things they are grateful for each day. Emphasize the team's function and mission and concentrate on how to connect, persevere, and progress.

Firsthand experiences and historical events can teach us about crisis management. Going through a crisis leaves deep scars on both people and institutions. As a result, it is critical to learn how to deal with a potential crisis as soon as possible. Crises are always associated with negativity and dramatization, resulting in elevated levels of stress.

However, crises provide an opportunity to gather experience and learn from them. As Albert Einstein once observed, "In the middle of difficulty lies opportunity," and after a crisis, individuals and organizations should emerge stronger than before. As a leader, convey both brutal honesty and credible hope that your team has the resources necessary to meet the threats they encounter every day: resolve, solidarity, strength, shared purpose, humanity, kindness, and resilience.

Moments of crisis tell a lot about leaders, and it is critical to understand who rose to the occasion, who faltered, and why. Consider how jobs will shift in the post-crisis era and whether you are positioning your own top leaders for success.

Finally, consider who you want at the table both during and after the crisis. Leaders who must navigate new and shifting priorities deserve assistance and coaching to maximize their performance.

Minor efforts in these areas can go a long way toward reaching this goal. It allows for growth and resiliency while revealing the genuine nature of the leader.

Volunteering during Times of Crisis

In times of catastrophe, international organizations, nonprofits, and governments frequently give humanitarian relief, such as food, water, shelter, medical supplies, and other necessary resources. External support can be lifesaving, especially when local resources are limited or unavailable as the crisis progresses.

Personal Log: Fort McMurray, Alberta, May 3, 2016: Through Hell!

I would like to express my sincere appreciation for the countless hours of volunteerism shown during times of crisis. In May 2016, as wildfires rapidly spread, forcing thousands of residents to evacuate their homes, local volunteers rose to the occasion.

During the immediate exodus from Fort McMurray, many residents had insufficient gas in their vehicles due to gas station closures. The immediate panic to escape the inferno led people to flee without planning. Families and pets, not having had the time to fill up their gas on the way south to Edmonton, had to abandon their cars on the side of the highway. Most relied on the kindness of other escapees to accommodate them in already overcrowded vehicles. Learning about this situation through various social media platforms, hundreds of volunteers from Edmonton and all the way from Calgary and other municipalities took it upon themselves to obtain gasoline in jerrycans and deliver it to stranded escapees. When offered payment, all these volunteers declined. Others carried water bottles, basic food, and supplies, driving to meet people they had never known but quickly forming a bond through shared acts of kindness and hope during those difficult hours.

When we found refuge in our different hotel properties, hundreds of compassionate souls brought food, clothing, toys, and supplies that not only improved the situation but also brought hope and cheerfulness when they were most needed. Volunteer organizations, community centres, and local churches opened their doors to provide emergency shelter to displaced individuals and families. Volunteers worked tirelessly to set up and manage these shelters, providing food, bedding, and emotional support to the evacuated, desperate citizens. They offered a sense of comfort and stability during a challenging time.

Community volunteers rallied together to collect and distribute essential supplies, such as food, water, clothing, toiletries, and other necessities.

As a pet owner myself, I commend all those involved in animal rescue and care. During the wildfires, volunteers played a crucial role in rescuing and caring for animals affected by the disaster. They helped evacuate pets and livestock, setting up temporary shelters for displaced animals and providing them with food, water, and medical attention. Veterinary professionals and animal welfare organizations also volunteered their services to support these efforts. Months after the crisis, I talked to a firefighter who had fought the Beast. When I asked him what the most challenging task for him had been, he recounted the terrible and haunting barking of abandoned dogs in houses burning to the ground, imagining the last thoughts of a dog wondering why their beloved owners had left them perilous to such a tragic fate.

Countless acts of generosity, valour, and commitment have given me hope when despair had me wondering if all was lost. In a crisis, people band together, realizing that they are all affected by the situation. This shared experience generates a sense of solidarity, resulting in collective motivation.

Individuals frequently feel an intense sense of empathy and compassion during a crisis. Witnessing others' suffering and hardships might arouse a strong urge to assist and support those in need. This increased empathy motivates people to offer their time, skills, and resources to make a positive difference.

I am extremely grateful to all the people who came to our aid. Individuals gain personal gratification and a sense of purpose from volunteering, particularly when assisting others in times of need. They understand the practical and significant difference they can make in the lives of others. The act of selflessly giving back to promote the well-being of other people provides deep satisfaction.

Crises frequently expose social, economic, and environmental challenges, shedding light on systemic imbalances and vulnerabilities that must be addressed. Volunteers see these situations as chances to effect constructive change, whether through immediate assistance or campaigning for long-term solutions. They recognize that volunteerism is vital to building a more resilient and equitable society.

For an effective response and recovery, crises necessitate a varied set of skills and resources. Volunteerism expresses the intrinsic human potential for compassion as well as the conviction in the power of collective action to overcome issues and develop stronger communities. Volunteering brings immeasurable gratitude in times of crisis.

Although a crisis has a massive impact on all victims, the brilliant light of hope that volunteers ignite makes the load less heavy for all who are experiencing these calamitous events. Their tremendous offer of love and concern towards us benefited myself, my family, the teams, and many others. Crises will continue to afflict us all, but volunteers will continue to rise in the face of adversity and demonstrate unwavering courage and respect for humankind.

God bless everyone and stay safe!

Pictures

May 1, 2016, 3:00 p.m. In the beginning.

May 2, 2016, 7:30 a.m. The calm before the storm.

From "Hell"

May 3, 2016, 1:30 p.m. Southside of town leaving the Radisson Hotel.

May 3, 2016, 2:00 p.m. Wall of flame descending on the city.

May 3, 2016, 3:30 p.m. Leaving from home.

May 3, 2016, 3:45 p.m. Driving downtown.

May 3, 2016, 8:45 p.m. Leaving the inferno.

May 4, 2016, in Anzac refuge. Me and Jaxx, catching up on sleep.

May 20, 2016. The return.

To "High Water"

April 26, 2020. One of our hotel properties, The Merit Hotel.

April 26, 2020. Boating on Main Street.

Bibliography

Collins, Jim. *Good to Great: Why Some Companies Make the Leap . . . and Others Don't*. New York: HarperCollins Publishers, 2001.

Covey, Steven R. *The 7 Habits of Highly Effective People*. New York: Free Press, 1989.

DuBrin, Andrew J. *Foundations of Organizational Behavior: An Applied Perspective*. Hoboken, New Jersey: Prentice Hall, 1984.

Goleman, Daniel. *Emotional Intelligence: Why It Can Matter More than IQ*. New York: Bantam Books, 1995.

Goodwin, Doris Kearns. *Leadership in Turbulent Times*. New York: Simon & Schuster, 2018.

Kouzes, James M., and Barry Z. Posner. *The Leadership Challenge*. 3rd ed. Hoboken, New Jersey: Jossey-Bass, 2002.

Lencioni, Patrick M. *The Five Dysfunctions of a Team*. 20th anniversary ed. Hoboken, New Jersey: Jossey-Bass, 2002.

Marcus, Leonard J., Eric McNulty, Joseph M. Henderson, and Barry C. Dorn. *You're It: Crisis, Change, and How to Lead When It Matters Most*. New York: Hachette Book Group, 2021.

Maxwell, John C. *The 21 Irrefutable Laws of Leadership*. 10th anniversary ed. Nashville: Thomas Nelson, 2007.

McChrystal, Stanley, Tantum Collins, David Silverman, and Chris Fussell. *Team of Teams: New Rules of Engagement for a Complex World*. New York: Portfolio, 2015.

Nordin, Kathya N. "Making Sense of Leaders' Perceptions about Effectiveness in Communication during a Crisis." Master thesis, Mid Sweden University, 2020. http://www.diva-portal.org/smash/get/diva2:1535125/FULLTEXT01.pdf.

Pfeifer, Joseph. *Crisis Leadership: The Art of Adapting to Extreme Events.* Harvard Kennedy School. PCL Discussion Paper Series, March 2013. https://www.hks. harvard.edu/sites/default/files/centers/research-initiatives/crisisleadership/ files/Pfeifer%20Crisis%20Leadership—March%2020%202013.pdf.

Raue, Steve, Suk-Han Tang, Christian Weiland, and Claas Wenzik. *The GRPI Model: An Approach for Team Development.* Berlin-Mitte: Systemic Excellence Group, 2013.

www.ingramcontent.com/pod-product-compliance
Lightning Source LLC
Chambersburg PA
CBHW031049180526
45163CB00002BA/752